INTELLECTUAL MODERNISM OF SHIBLĪ NU'MĀNĪ

"The historic flux into which every phenomenon is dissolved cannot yield the *norms* for faith and action, yet life without such norms does not seem worth living."

from Joachim Wach's
The Comparative Study of Religions

Intellectual Modernism of SHIBLI NU'MÃNÎ

AN EXPOSITION OF HIS RELIGIOUS AND POLITICAL IDEAS

Mrs. Mehr Afroz Murad

KITAB BHAVAN
New Delhi-2 (India)

KITAB BHAVAN
Publishers, Distributors, Exporters & Importers
1784, Kalan Mahal, Darya Ganj,
New Delhi - 1100 02 (India)

Phones : (91-11) 23277392/93, 23274686, 32906494
Fax : (91-11) 23263383
Website : www.kitabbhavan.com
Email : nasri@vsnl.com
: nusrat@bol.net.in

First Published in India ... 1996
2nd Edition 2009

ISBN : 81-7151-216-X
Book Code No. : I000160

Printed & Published in India by :
Nusrat Ali Nasri for KITAB BHAVAN
1784, Kalan Mahal, Darya Ganj,
New Delhi - 1100 02 [India]

TO MY PARENTS

Foreword

The man who is the subject of this book is one of the foremost figures of modern Muslim India but one whose individuality, depth and manysidedness have yet to be properly appreciated. At once a scholar of formidable learning as well as a thinker of independence of mind, he left behind him an extensive body of writings very wide ranging in scope and of great interest. Among them are essays that not only contribute to understanding the man and his age but which are also of much value in themselves and which merit far more attention than they have so far gained. Among the strengths of the present volume is its demonstration of the multi-facetedness of Shiblī. Thus, it serves to correct a distorted image by presenting a more rounded view of his imposing personality than was previously available.

Almost every writer on the evolution of the Muslim community in the Indo-Pakistan subcontinent during the past hundred years has found it necessary to devote some pages to a consideration of Shiblī and his thought; he is not, however, well known outside the circles of those who have specialised in the study of Indian Islam. The approaches to him in the literature have been dominated by two considerations: (1) the desire to see him in the light of the developments among the Muslims which led to the partition of the sub-continent and the emergence of Pakistan and (2) the desire to assess his contribution to the intellectual evolution of the Muslim community in the modern period more generally, that is, to evaluate the effect he may have had in changing the ways Muslims have thought and acted in regard to their modern situation. In neither of these respects did Shiblī make an important mark on his contemporaries, and it is this fact which, perhaps, more than anything else, accounts for the relative neglect he has suffered at the hands of students of Islam in modern India. As the present volume shows with great clarity, Shiblī was not actually involved in the political stirrings that began to agitate the Indian Muslim community toward the end of the nineteenth century, nor did his attention focus primarily on the issues that arose from the burgeoning desire among Muslims to rehabilitate the fortunes of the community, socially, economically, politically and militarily. If he is judged from the standpoint of the Muslim nationalism that produced Pakistan, his contribution may appear to be unimportant and his efforts to have been misguided. If he be judged for his stance toward the problems that were central to the heroes of Muslim renaissance in modern times, whether in India or elsewhere, he may be seen as irrelevant or even as obstructive to reform efforts. Most scholarly opinion has viewed him as a partially enlightened conservative, but none the less essentially an upholder of the Islamic *status quo* in India, laying emphasis upon those of his writings which celebrate the glories of Islamic history and upon the nature of the education offered in the Nadwat al-'Ulamā' in contrast to Aligarh. Such judgments are inadequate, principally because they are made according to criteria that do not fit Shiblī's case. In his time Shiblī was concerned with matters other than those which subsequent events have raised to the position of first importance. If he is to be understood for what he was and for the values he may have to transmit, efforts must be made to view him in his own terms and to penetrate into the peculiar nature of his own mental set. The present volume is a determined effort to achieve these goals. By going beyond the perspectives characteristic of the majority of scholars, the work has contributed in a substantial way to a more enlightened grasp of Shiblī and to a fuller appreciation of his contribution to Islamic thought. It goes far toward righting the balance in the studies devoted to him through underlining his complexity, the highly individual nature of his preoccupations, the variety of his concerns and even the occasional inconsistency of his thought. The result is a more vivid and more valid picture of Shiblī as a man.

One of the important emphases that emerges in the work at hand is Shiblī's concern with the rethinking of fundamental Islamic theology. Unlike many other Muslim leaders in recent times, he both recognised and acknowledged a threat to his religious faith from science and the modern intellectual milieu, and also unlike others his response did not come as defensive apologetics but as a creative reconsideration of the Islamic heritage in the light of the problems posed by science. The problem of an adequate theological stance in our difficult age was of deep personal concern to him; the issues were rooted in a keenly felt puzzlement of mind and a genuine personal need to gain a satisfying intellectual grasp of his religious faith. He was thus involved with the philosophy of religion, one of the small group of significant modern Muslim thinkers to have been so. Although one may not be satisfied with Shiblī's resolution of the problems he discussed, and that of science and religion in particular, the very fact of a first-rate thinker's having seen the importance of these problems and given himself to energetic thought about them is itself of much significance. This side of his thought deserves greatly increased attention, and hopefully it will serve as a stimulus to others to follow his lead. It is at once an expression of confidence in the strength and richness of the Islamio heritage that enable it to withstand close investigation and adaptation, as well as a demonstration of an inquiring and modern spirit. For Shiblī there was no cause for fear in subjecting his Islamic faith to close scrutiny, only the irresistible drive to bring his religious commitments and his intellectual convictions into accord.

The debt of the scholarly community to the author of this book is due not only for the first full-length study in English of a compelling personality and for the care and thoroughness with which the work has been done, but also for the liveliness of the style in which the whole is presented. Mrs Murad has achieved a compact presentation of her subject in language that is clear, forceful and readable, making her book a pleasure to read. The keenness of her own mind and the pithiness of her expression as well as her independence in following where her evidence has led her are reminiscent of Shiblī himself. Her achievement should be an encouragement to others and a proof of what persistence and hard work will accomplish even when the circumstances in which one must work are not favourable.

CHARLES J. ADAMS

Institute of Islamic Studies
McGill University
Montreal, P.Q.
June 1976

Preface

This study of a single individual's share in and contribution to the intellectual developments in modern Indian Islam was originally a Master's thesis submitted to the Institute of Islamic Studies, McGill University, Montreal, Canada, in 1973. It is now being presented to the general readership with very slight changes only. The study assumes much and offers little in the way of a total interpretation of the phenomenon of modernism in Indian Islam, except perhaps that it emphasises the role of ideas in it. Though conceived and executed quite independently of them, the study turned out more and more to corroborate and substantiate, to exemplify and amplify the interpretations (not mutually exclusive) already presented by earlier and worthier students of modern Indian Islam, especially Professors Wilfred Cantwell Smith, Fazlur Rahman and Aziz Ahmad. As it stands now, it is rather an extended footnote to the works of the aforementioned authors in this field. The present writer's only real claim to originality lies with regard to the subject of this study himself. She has studied Shiblī Nu'mānī at length in relation particularly to his religious and political writings, and has tried to bring to light, or rather to life, certain moribund aspects of Shiblī's manifold intellectual personality. In the process she has been able to present a vastly modified picture especially of Shiblī's religious thinking, and has generally shown that Shiblī had a much more modern mind than he is usually credited with.

Before we try and place Shiblī within the context of early modern Islam in India, a few words of qualification seem essential. Shiblī's was, perhaps more than anyone else's among his contemporaries, a variegated, protean mind. This quality of mind may be attributed to his restless, mercurial soul, to the changing pressures of his times and environs, to the evolution in his thinking or to mere inconsistency in his thought. The fact, however, remains that Shiblī is a man difficult to categorise, label and pigeon-hole. Not only were his views undergoing change with the passage of time, but he was quite capable of adopting intellectual attitudes of an essentially different ethos at one and the same time. On the question, for instance, of a proper system of education for Indian Muslims, Shiblī ended up by being almost a reactionary reformer, which was a far cry from his earlier, more liberal, views on education. Or, for instance, in his main field of intellectual endeavour, the Islamic past, especially in its cultural-institutional aspect, Shiblī remained throughout a romanticising apologist. On the other hand, in matters of theology, law and politics he showed an increasingly realistic, modern liberal tendency. And it is these last three spheres of his thought, or rather the liberal-modernist strands in his overall thinking, with which we have deliberately concerned ourselves in this study. This clarification was necessary in order not only to give due recognition to the various facets of Shiblī's thought, but also to avoid an exaggerated impression about the modernism of it. Modernism was merely one, although greatly significant, piece in the mosaic of his thought.

Shiblī may not be a modernist through and through, but we contend that, compared to the traditional, the modernist element in his thought is perhaps more characteristically representative of the spirit of his mind. What we are trying to suggest is that Shiblī was virtually forced into taking defensive and reactionary positions in certain aspects and at certain levels of his thought. But it was against his grain, and against the liberal progressive spirit of his mental make-up. (Had he been spared the "mordant and derisive" attacks on Islam by Christian missionaries and early Orientalists, and been exposed to Western thought and methodology in pleasanter circumstances, Shiblī would have made a much more scientific historian and liberal educationist.) It was some such perception of Shiblī's intellectual temperament which made his friend, admirer and critic, Mahdī Ḥasan, remark that "Shiblī was the first Greek born in [Muslim] India". This judgment is sufficiently borne out by Shiblī's manifest rationalism, humanism and liberalism in handling the problems of theology, law and politics in Islam. (Indeed, if Shiblī had gained direct and frequent access to the Europenn studies in religion and philosophy, he might have improved the quality of his work on Islamic theology. His was an enterprising soul, imbued with that spirit of learning which characterised the early European Humanists. It is a pity that his main source of Western thought was Farīd Wajdī or at best a few polemical translations.)

In spite of the foregoing, Shiblī has generally emerged in the minds of Muslim posterity in India as a traditionalist, a defender of Islamic faith and history and the author of *Sīrat al-Nabī* and *Al-Fārūq*. Even to Smith he is "an example of a fairly conservative mind" or at best an "orthodox rationaliser". This image of Shiblī can partly be explained by suggesting, as Smith has done in the case of Shiblī's Egyptian contemporary, Muḥammad 'Abduh, that the liberal element is only partially incorporated in the finished product of his work, and that his work lacks systematic exposition. Shiblī's disciples and devotees also played a large role in building up this image, especially his Boswell, Sayyid Sulaymān Nadwī, who ignored or explained away the liberal, progressive elements, and accentuated the conservative and traditional elements in his thought. In fact, Sulaymān Nadwī's biography of Shiblī can be justly described as an attempt to paint Shiblī in orthodox colours. Even if there had been no deliberate suppression of Shiblī's modernism, there was still no guarantee that the Muslim self image would not have unconsciously trimmed Shiblī to its liking. It could not very well shelve and forget his works—something it did to Sayyid Aḥmad Khān's writings—for they were more than gratifying for Muslim self-respect and were part of the Muslim defence mechanism.

Shiblī was not primarily or even essentially a reformist, at least not in any overt sense. Most certainly he was not a revivalist-purificationist. To say this is to say really a lot about him. First of all it sets him apart from what Fazlur Rahman calls the pre-modernist reform movement, as it distinguishes him from the continuation of this particular reform phenomenon in modern times. (This is not to deny that some of his writings may have indirectly helped the revivalist tendency by portraying the periods of 'Umar I and the Prophet in glowing, nostalgic tones.) Shiblī does not summon his fellow Indian Muslims back to pristine Islam in terms of the Qur'ān and the *Sunnah* and the practice or doctrines of the earliest generations of the Muslims. He does not go over and beyond the historic Muslim community as it evolved through the centuries. He does not reject the accommodations and cultural richness of medieval Islam, or repudiate as such the authority of medieval schools of Islamic law. Not particularly concerned with the socio-moral reconstruction of the contemporary Islamic society in India, he was not emphasising the *sharī'ah* or its implementation. He was not an activist (indeed, he interpreted *jihād* in purely defensive terms), nor did he have any idea of an Islamic state in abstraction, or of an Islamic system of government as an instrument for implementing the *sharī'ah.* He was not one of the people of Tradition who appeared to save the Sunnī orthodox formulation of Islam. He was not even reacting against sufism, or rejecting the intellectualist trends in Islam—the two banes of orthodoxy. Thus he was free from the influence of pre-modernist reform movements of India or of the Middle East, just as he was not under the influence of Ibn Taymīyyah, the medieval progenitor of these movements. Indeed, it would be most difficult to prove that even the ground of his modernist thinking was prepared by the pre-modernist reform phenomena. Unlike Afghānī, 'Abduh and Sayyid Aḥmad Khān, Shiblī did not come from a purificationist-reformist background and was not a reformer in the sense in which these three turned out to be. His writings are conspicuously free from calls for social reform; he was not concerned with society as such. He was not reacting to, or protesting against, the degeneration of Muslim society—except by the remotest implication,—nor was he engaged in remedying social evils and raising moral standards. Shiblī was an intellectualist first and an intellectualist last. His interest in educational reform was essentially an extension of his intellectualism; he wanted to produce better Muslim intellectuals. The most superficial comparison of *Al-Nadwah* with *Tahdhīb al-Akhlāq* will bring out this distinctive character of Shiblī's approach.

Smith's thesis that since Islam has been associated with power and success in history, and since the central expression of faith has been societal, therefore it was the community which felt threatened with the loss of power, and therefore the modern problem of Islam was to preserve the community, may be true in most cases, and at a deeper psychological and analytical level in all cases, of modern Muslim group and individual activity. However, it fails to take into account, in tangible terms, the case of a Muslim intellectual like Shiblī who was not so much worried about the threat to the community and the loss of power and prestige as he was worried about the truth and validity of his beliefs which were being threatened by modern science. To some modern Muslims, at least, science did not merely represent a new technology and industrial power, something to be acquired. Rather it meant a renewal of the problem of faith and reason, something to be faced—however imperfect their understanding of the implications of science for religion, and thus however inadequate the formulation of their answers to this problem. It is a measure of the importance which Shiblī attached to this question—and thus indicative of his somewhat different outlook on the modern problem of Islam—that the number of books and articles which he wrote on theology greatly outnumbered those written on law and were surpassed only by his works on history and literature. Although he took up law as an object of his thought, his attitude towards it appears to be rather negative, while he hardly seems to consider politics a valid field for religious thinking. Its defensive note notwithstanding, Shiblī was, to a considerable degree, concerned with the intellectual reformulation of Islam as a faith; he was trying to redefine the contents and methods of faith—primarily under the impact of the West.

Shiblī belonged to a diverse group of Islamic liberals who flourished briefly about the turn of the present century. "There are two major elements from within the past Islamic tradition from which a contribution to liberalism could be drawn: philosophy and Sufism," says Smith. Shiblī drew upon both of them for his liberal reinterpretation of Islam. The mere fact that, contrary to the usual practice of Muslim thinkers, Shiblī was giving positive importance, within the Islamic scheme of things, to theology as compared to law or politics, is a sufficient indication of what he would seek from within the past Islamic tradition. The formal rationalism of the *falāsifah* and the *mutakallimīn*, especially the Mu'tazilites, would naturally be the single most important asset in Shiblī's revision of Islamic ideology. The intellectual sufism served more or less the same purpose. It should be noted that Shiblī was not a sufi either by training or by temperament, but was attracted by, and made use of, the mystical rationalism of the sufis. Scarcely less liberating influences on Shiblī's mind emanated from his being a historian and man of letters and culture. That is the reason why, despite his religious learning, the title of *'ālim* seems somewhat incongruous when applied to him. The nearest medieval parallel to a man of his broad accomplishments would perhaps be an Abbasid or a Mamlūk *kātib*, not discounting the secular spirit which characterised the class of the *kuttāb*. In spite of the liberating influences of his personal humanism and his re-embracing of the rationalist strand in the historical tradition, in the present writer's opinion, the direct or "efficient" cause of Shiblī's liberalism was the impact of Western thought, to which he was first exposed during his association with Aligarh. (The question of the precise channels of transmission of Western ideas to Shiblī is not really important—though there were several such channels—since these ideas and their presuppositions were, so to say, in the air.) Shiblī's drawing upon the past Islamic tradition was, we believe, in the way of the "material" or "formal" cause of his liberalism. Very much a man of the present, he had, however, a very strong sense of the past. Like 'Abduh, he "welcomed Western liberalism in fact if not in name, and sought to incorporate it into or harmonise it with Islam". This harmonising, we believe, was fairly creative. Shiblī was groping for a new synthesis. He would not merely prove that revealed Islam and scientific reason were mutually compatible but, in the process, would also generate a new evaluation, a new orientation and a new vision of Islam.

Our choice of Shiblī as the subject of this biographical excursion into the intellectual history of modern Indian Islam is warranted by several factors, starting with the assumption that perhaps no other history will lend itself to biographical treatment more suitably and fruitfully than the history of ideas. To begin with, it was prompted by sheer fascination with his colourful and complex personality which stood out in a group of extraordinary but basically plain and linear personalities like Sayyid Aḥmad Khān, Ḥālī and Chirāgh 'Alī. Perhaps it was this kaleidoscopic and enigmatic quality which led different people to view him differently, atomistically and conveniently as poet, lover, literary critic, historian, educationist, pan-Islamist and ***mutakallim***. But all of them generally missed Shiblī the liberal religious thinker. They missed the essential rationalist, humanist impulse of the man which ran particularly through his religious and political thought. Indeed, nobody seems to have taken him seriously as a religious thinker. Characteristically, Smith comes closest to doing this, but even he suffers from the usual Orientalistic obsession with apologetics, which is quite all right, but only up to a point. It should not be allowed to blind us to the streak of creative modernity present in Shiblī's thought. Indeed, Aziz Ahmad goes a little bit too far when he declares that "the cast of his mind is essentially medieval". To bring the neglected modernist side of his thought into relief is another reason for our choice of Shiblī as the subject of this study.

In point of fact, no aspect of Shiblī's thought, and for that matter perhaps even of his life, has yet been studied properly. (A certain Z. 'Umar's Doctoral dissertation on Shiblī's romanticism, submitted to London University, may prove to be the exception; but we have not seen it to be able to make a definite assessment.) In English, Smith's treatment of Shiblī in ***Modern Islam in India*** is perhaps still the best, and Aziz Ahmad's summary of his ideas in ***Islamic Modernism in India and Pakistan***, the lengthiest. One may go so far as to suggest that Western scholarship has generally ignored Shiblī, at least in comparison to Sayyid Aḥmad Khān and Ameer Ali. The situation at home is just the reverse of it. Shiblī has almost totally eclipsed Ameer Ali and vies with Sayyid Aḥmad Khān in terms of the attention of local scholarship. This is evidenced by the number of monographs written about him, special issues of journals dedicated to him and even doctoral theses done on him. But this attention is mostly misdirected. It has developed personal, partisan tones instead of evolving into dispassionate inquiries; or it has been wasted on insignificant and trivial matters. This state of affairs was precipitated by Sayyid Sulaymān Nadwī's biographical work on his master, *Ḥayāt-i Shiblī*, and generally revolved around two themes: Shiblī's dissent from Sayyid Aḥmad Khān and the Aligarh School and his so-called affair with 'Aṭīyyah Begam Fayḍī. *Ḥayāt-i Shiblī*, an otherwise monumentally informative work, tried to make almost a saint out of Shiblī at the expense of Sayyid Aḥmad Khān and almost totally suppressed his relations with 'Aṭīyyah Begam—none of which Shiblī would probably approve of if he were living. A number of works appeared to counter these two points, and poor Shiblī was turned into a hotbed of passionate controversy. While it would be difficult, perhaps even futile, to make a selection from devotional literature on him, the most representative of the anti-Shiblī writings are the works by Muḥammad Amīn Zubayrī and Shaykh Muḥammad Ikrām, especially their *Dhikr-i Shiblī* and *Shiblī Nāmah* respectively Ikrām has, however, made amends in his recent *Yādgār-i Shiblī* (Lahore, 1971), a general monograph on the life and works of Shiblī. Although a definite improvement on his earlier work both in its scope and treatment, and comparatively balanced in its appraisal of Shiblī's character and achievements, it is still rather personal and partisan in its basic approach and undertones. It does not really develop into an inquiry at once dispassionate and sympathetic, except perhaps where it deals with Shiblī's works, which constitutes its more significant portion One would expect a more meaningful and profound treatment of Shiblī in the two doctoral dissertations written on him. But one unpublished dissertation, presented by Sakhī Aḥmad Hāshimī to the Sind University in 1966, with the high-sounding title "Shiblī Kā Dhihnī Irtiqā'," is hardly more than a chronology of his life and writings. The other, published dissertation, *Shiblī—Ek Dabistān*, submitted to Aligarh University around 1945 by Aftab Aḥmad Ṣiddīqī under the title *Shiblī Awr Un Kī Taṣānīf*, is relatively a better attempt in that it is a topical treatment of various facets of Shiblī's literary personality. However, it is superficial and also suffers from the author's devotion to Shiblī. Much more valuable are the occasional articles contributed to various journals, especially to the special Shiblī issues of *Al-Baṣīr* (1957), *Ṣabā'* (1958) and *Adīb* (1960). This dearth of serious writing on Shiblī was another factor which prompted us to choose him as the subject of this study. Perhaps it would not be too presumptuous to hope that in conjunction with Ikrām's *Yādgār-i Shiblī*, Z. 'Umar's work on Shiblī's romanticism and Anīs Aḥmad's Ph.D. dissertation on the historical methodology of Shiblī and Ameer Ali being prepared for submission to the Temple University, Philadelphia, this brief study will contribute to a more serious and significant discussion of Shiblī.

I owe this study, from start to finish, to four adorable persons, but for whom this study just would not be. It was the ever-ready-to-help Dr Ẓafar Isḥāq Anṣārī, Associate Professor of History, University of Petroleum and Minerals, Dhahrān, who first recommended Shiblī as a promising subject for research, and even suggested a preliminary outline of the work. He was also good enough to give a quick look-over to the final draft of this study. If he finds that I have radically digressed from the original scheme, he has only to blame himself for not being around when this study was being done. It was the always-to-the-point Professor Niyazi Berkes of the Institute of Islamic Studies, McGill University, Montreal, who advised me to forget about the life of Shiblī and concentrate on his thought. He was also kind enough to discuss with me various problems of a general nature connected with this study. It was the never-give-up Dr Charles J. Adams, Professor and Director of the Institute of Islamic Studies, McGill University, and my research adviser, who waited for such a long time for so small a piece of research. When at last it materialised, he painstakingly went through the first draft of all the three chapters page by page and sentence by sentence. He not only corrected them language-wise, but also suggested a number of improvements in their contents. If I could not fully follow up all these suggestions, it was only because I was too lazy to do it. I still hope to incorporate them in some subsequent revision of the work. It was my not-quite-satisfied husband, Hasan Q̱āsim Murād, who not only helped me render many an Urdu passages into English and generally assisted me in preparing the first draft, but was constantly around to drive me to work. Nevertheless, he believes that I have been rather unfair to Shiblī in that I have overstressed the modernist note in his thought. For all I know he just may have a point there. My gratitude to these gentlemen cannot be adequately expressed in words, at least not in a language as alien as English. I am also grateful to Father Böwering, my colleague at the Institute of Islamic Studies, McGill University, and Dr Manzur Ahmad, Associate Professor of Philosophy, University of Karachi, for reading the first chapter and making several valuable suggestions and criticisms.

The library staff of the Institute of Islamic Studies, McGill University, especially Mr Muzaffar Ali and Miss Salwa Farahian, who went out of their way to help me find books and articles, deserve my especial thanks. Thanks are also due to Mr M. Ashraf Darr who not only edited and marked the script for press in his expert way, but also saw to the printing of the book with his characteristic meticulousness.

But for the financial assistance arranged by the Institute of Islamic Studies, McGill University, only God and Miss Eve Yuile, the efficient Secretary of the Institute, would know from where, it would not have been possible for me to go abroad and do post-graduate research at such a distinguished University as McGill. I deeply appreciate this act of generosity.

I also want to take this opportunity to express my deepest gratitude to my mother who, despite her old age and failing health, took the very best care of my children in Karachi, and made it possible for me to stay in Montreal.

I must also offer thanks to those wonderful people who took active interest in seeing this thesis published: to Dr Adams for suggesting the idea of its publication and consenting to write a Foreword to it; to Dr Manzur Ahmad for introducing it to Professor M. Saeed Sheikh, Director,

Institute of Islamic Culture, Lahore; and, lastly, to Professor M. Saeed Sheikh for considering it worthy enough to be published by the Institute of Islamic Culture and executing its publication with such care, concern and despatch.

Lastly, a few words about the system of transliteration, bibliography and appendix. The letters of the Urdu alphabet, including the Persian-Arabic letters, are transliterated as follows (in Urdu alphabetical order):

ا	a	د	d	ض	ḍ	م	m
ب	b	ڈ		ط	ṭ	ن	n
پ	p	ذ	dh	ظ	ẓ	ں	
ت	t	ر	r	ع	‘	و	w
ٹ		ڑ		غ	gh	ہ	h
ث	th	ز	z	ف	f	ء	’
ج	j	ژ	zh	ق	q	ی	y
چ	ch	س	s	ک	k	ے	
ح	ḥ	ش	sh	گ	g		
خ	kh	ص	ṣ	ل	l		

The vowels used are a i u (short), ā ī ū (long), ā (*alif maqṣūrah*), ’ā (*alif mamdūdah*); and, for the dipthongs, aw and ay. The Arabic article is transcribed *al*. The *iḍāfah* is indicated by i and *tā’ marbūṭah* by ah or at.

The bibliography consists only of the works referred to in the footnotes.

Preface

Since the study does not contain the conventional chapter on the subject's life, it was thought advisable to add a chronological bio bibliography comprising the main events of Shiblī's life and his chief works—as an Appendix.

Mehr Afroz Murad

Karachi
1 May 1976

Table of Contents

I

Rationalist Theology

(1)

"Today we are, as before, in need of a modern theology (*'ilm al-kalām*), whereby we should either refute doctrines of modern sciences, or undermine their foundations, or show that they are in conformity with Islam."[1]

Thus did Sayyid Aḥmad Khān respond to the question of the relationship between reason and faith in Islam raised anew with unprecedented acuteness due to the situation—economic-political, psychological-cultural and intellectual-religious—obtaining in India in the last half of the nineteenth century. A new phase of assimilation, rejection and adjustment had begun for Indian Islam, both as a tradition and as a faith. Without denying the partial validity of the argument that a change in material conditions preceded the ideological adaptation and may even have been the cause of it, and without also denying the general truth of the statement that the modern challenge was primarily to the social institutions of Islam, one must recognise

1. Quoted in Fazlur Rahman, *Islam*, p. 217.

that on a purely intellectual level problems were also raised for specific religious beliefs of Islam directly by modern Western philosophical and scientific theories. The whole problem indeed was raised to a more general level, whether faith and reason can accommodate one another. These problems had been discussed for centuries in Islam by Muslim thinkers, but had acquired a new dimension and assumed a new quality under the impact of the nineteenth-century rationalism and scientific developments. The conflict was not any longer just between religion and thought, but between religion and scientific thought. The new scientific worldview had its own claims for recognition. This was the problem, both in its specific and general implications, to which Sayyid Aḥmad Khān and other late nineteenth-century Indian Muslim thinkers addressed themselves. In so doing they were not so much aiming at producing scientific thought as they were trying to sove a situation —to save their religion from the relentless encroachment of modern thought by finding a *modus vivendi* between the two.[2]

It seems ironic that in Muslim India the first outstanding person to feel the need of a new *kalām* was Sayyid Aḥmad Khān who was himself largely responsible for deliberately introducing Western sciences among the Indian Muslims. What Sayyid

2. Cf. ibid., pp. 214 f.; *idem*. "Revival and Reform in Islam," *Cambridge History of Islam*, II, 644-46. See also Nadav Safran, *Egypt in Search of Political Community*, p. 2.

Aḥmad Khān actually did was that he showed that Islam was in conformity with modern sciences; he did not refute them, nor did he undermine their foundations. The means Sayyid Aḥmad Khān adopted towards that end was essentially to re-interpret the Qur'ān. He laid down certain principles for his *tafsīr*, the most central of which was that there could not possibly be any contradiction between the *work* of God (Nature) and the *word* of God (Qur'ān). If there were such a contradiction between the two, he argued, it would necessarily follow that the word of God is false, since the work of God is undeniably self-evident; and since the word of God cannot be false, therefore both have to be uniform (*muttaḥid*).[3] It was perhaps only natural that Sayyid Aḥmad Khān should equate human reason (*insānī 'aql*), which he regarded as the sole arbiter and harmoniser between the two,[4] with the nineteenth-century European scientists' view of nature and its laws. This in effect meant that Sayyid Aḥmad Khān turned the contemporary scientific worldview into the overriding principle of the interpretation of the Qur'ān. Sayyid's Aḥmad Khān's task of reinterpreting the Qur'ānic concepts and formulating a modern theology may or may not have been made easier by this principle, but it surely cut him loose from the orthodox tradition and drove him to the

3. Sayyid Aḥmad Khān, *Taḥrīr fī Uṣūl al-Tafsīr*, p. 6.
4. Ibid.

medieval Muslim philosophers—something which not only cost him in terms of popularity, but also prevented his *kalām* from becoming the representative expression of Islamic faith.[5] His colleague Shiblī, who also felt the need of a new science of *kalām*, most probably taking his cue from Sayyid Aḥmad Khān, tried to propose a different solution to the problem. What was his solution and how far was he successful in his venture?—we shall try to see in the following pages. Shiblī expounded his views on the subject mainly in a series of four monographs entitled *'Ilm al-Kalām*, *Al Ghazālī*, *Al-Kalām*, and *Sawāniḥ Mawlānā Rūm*. "Typical of his method, and his whole viewpoint," the first two and the last works are essentially historical-biographical. In the third he expressly propounds his theology for today.

(2)

In conscious disagreement with Sayyid Aḥmad Khān as to the nature of the need of a new *kalām* and, therefore, the nature of the response itself, Shiblī in his *Al-Kalām* starts with a harsh attack on Sayyid Aḥmad Khān's position in these words:

"It is being claimed today that the old philosophy could not destroy religion since it was based on conjectures and

5. Fazlur Rahman, *Islam*, p. 218 ; *idem*, "Revival and Reform in Islam," op. cit., II, 645 f.; Aziz Ahmad, *Islamic Modernism*, pp. 41 ff.; W. C. Smith, *Islam in Modern History*, p. 74.

hypothetical assumptions (*qiyāsāt awr ẓanniyāt*); but since modern philosophy is based wholly on experiment and observation (*tajribah awr mushāhadah*), religion cannot survive in opposition to it. This is a common cry which having once arisen from Europe has resounded all over the world. But we must discern carefully the element of fallacy (*mughālaṭah*) which has entered into this factuality (*wāqi'īyyat*)."

Shiblī then went on to make a distinction between modern science and modern philosophy. He said that the Greek *falsafah* denoted an aggregate of various disciplines including physics, astrology, theology and metaphysics; but Europe very correctly divided it into two parts: matters which were definitely and indisputably established on the basis of observation and experiment were called science, and those which were beyond the grasp of experiment and observation were called philosophy. Shiblī finds no conflict between science and religion. Indeed, according to him, they have nothing to do with each other, their subject-matters and scopes being absolutely separate. How many elements are there? What are the ingredients of water? What is the weight of air, and the speed of light? These and such other matters belong to science and are of no concern to religion, says Shiblī. The questions with which religion deals, and which cannot be touched by science, are: Does God exist? Is there another life after death? Is there any reality of good and evil? Is there reward and punishment? The most that even materialist scientists have claimed concerning these things is that since they are outside the realm of experiment and observation, therefore they neither know about them nor believe in them. But "third-rate materialists" and "the short-sighted," Shiblī says, "take the non-existence of knowledge to mean the knowledge of non-existence". The confusion arises, Shiblī goes on to say, when either of the two, science or religion, steps into the realm of the other. It was such trespass that led to unbelief in Europe where the scope of religion was so much enlarged that no scientific question remained outside its jurisdiction. Consequently, the priests denounced all kinds of scientific inventions and discoveries as acts of heresy and apostasy. Giving a brief description of the Inquisition Shiblī concludes that this development was peculiar to Christian Europe where religion was identified with the superstitions of the priests, and knowledge and reality regarded as opposed to it. But Islam, Shiblī maintains, is in no such danger, since it had declared in the very beginning that "you are more knowledgeable about the affairs of the world (*antum a'lamu bi umūri dunyākum*)". Despite the widespread practice among Muslims of charging persons with unbelief for petty matters, no one was ever charged with unbelief because of scientific investigations and discoveries. Shiblī quotes Shāh Walī Allāh to the effect that the Prophets' only concern is the refinement of morals (*tahdhīb al-akhlāq*) and they do not involve themselves in explaining natural causation. His conclusion is that the domain of Prophecy is separate from that of nature.[6]

On this somewhat theoretical-cum-historical level, Shiblī dealt with the problem of science versus religion and brought Islam forth from the confrontation apparently unscathed. As for philosophy, Shiblī maintained that there are scores of mutually disagreeing philosophical schools in Europe today, which sometimes come into conflict with religion. Since, however, they do not propound established truths, they do not constitute any danger for religion. In a lighter vein he suggests that religion might well sit back and watch with equanimity while these schools fight out among themselves.[7]

Once Shiblī had dissociated religion from science and put it into the same genre as philosophy in so far as both dealt with matters beyond observation and experiment, all that was required to be done, as the sub-title of his *Al-Kalām* reads, was to "affirm the tenets of Islam against contemporary philosophy". But this task was easier described than done. In actual practice, he did not—indeed he could not—rest with this stated position. The neat and clear line of demarcation between science on the one hand and religion and philosophy on the other suffered a major shortcoming. Science did not consist merely of observed and tested

6. *Al-Kalām*, pp. 7-15.

7. Ibid., pp. 7, 11.

facts, and philosophy was not speculation pure and simple. Science, when it dealt with questions of a general nature, took on the nature of philosophy. Philosophy in turn was deeply impressed by, and in many respects heavily based upon, the results of scientific activity. Whichever way one looked, science was there; and religion, inasmuch as it claimed to be a rational activity, could not remain just a disinterested spectator. Shiblī must have been aware of all this since at one place he went so far as to admit that in comparison with Greek *falsafah*, "the majority of the dicta of modern philosophy are based on realities and actualities".[8] But far more important and interesting is his own advertent or inadvertent blurring of the distinction between science and philosophy. At two different places, he uses the word "philosophy" to include the scientific theories, as we shall presently see. The quarrel was not really about the simple facts of science. Although it was task enough to convince the generality of Muslims as well as the *'ulamā'* that the elements had been proven to number more than four and that religion, in any case, was not involved positively or negatively in such matters,[9] this was not the point at issue. The fundamental issue arose where the so-called laws of science or nature, in so far as they proposed, explicitly or implicitly, alter-

8. *Maqālāt*, VII, 29.
9. Ibid., p. 38; Sayyid Sulaymān Nadwī, *Ḥayāt*, pp. 390 f.

nate answers to the ultimate questions, became a philosophy and a religion unto themselves and clashed with revelational worldview. Shiblī had to define his position with respect to these "laws" if he ever hoped to have religion reinstated and accepted as a rationally respectable system.

He went about his objective in two stages or at two levels. First, he emphasised the element of speculation and uncertainty involved in scientific theorising. At one place he cited the varying opinions of certain European scientists on the nature of the soul as a proof of their speculative character, and then asked rhetorically: "Can it be claimed on the basis of these [opinions] that the modern sciences have proven the soul non-existent?"[10] At another place he expresses himself in these words:

"A very important point is that philosophy, be it ethical, theological, or [pertaining to] perception of the realities of the universe [natural?] is not something sensible and self-evident. The present-day branches of philosophy in the Western countries, though they are easily understandable and more appealing to the mind, are not definite and absolute. The only proof of their correctness and actuality is that their dicta go to one's heart. But if one were bent upon denying them, they cannot be proved by irrefutable evidences. One of the great doctrines of modern philosophy is evolution which is propounded by Darwin . . . ; this doctrine is firmly established according to almost all the philosophers. But all of its proofs boil down to this: the creation of the universe in this particular manner is apparently more reasonable (*qarīn-i qiyās*)."[11]

10. *Al-Kalām*, pp. 10 f.

11. *Sawāniḥ*, pp. 95 f.

But Shiblī did not stop here. He went further and questioned the finality of the laws of nature themselves. Have all the laws of nature been determined? Is it certain that the things which we regard as the law of nature are really the law of nature?—he asks.[12] In the same vein he continues elsewhere:

> "No doubt philosophy means that one should discover the law of nature, the chain of cause and effect in the whole of universe. But the development of philosophy depends on not being content with the present findings; rather, evernew investigations should be carried out with a view to knowing if the chain we have affirmed is not wrong and whether there is not another law of nature in its stead."[13]

Thus, science and philosophy/religion may not be so unconcerned with one another as they were made out to be in the beginning, but Shiblī still was able to find a way to avoid the consequences of the intrusion of science into the realm of religion. Briefly put, he discovered the means whereby he could accommodate the supernatural elements in Islam with science or nature. That was perhaps all that really mattered. He had to find a way to explain "scientifically" or "naturally" the "other-worldly" in Islam. Once he did that, Shiblī not only surmounted the unsurmountable and crossed the main hurdle on his way to a rational Islam, but also set himself apart from Sayyid

12. *Al-Kalām*, p. 116.

13. *Sawāniḥ*, p. 157.

Aḥmad Khān in a rather fundamental way. Sayyid Aḥmad Khān had sacrificed the "irrational" in Islam at the altar of science and nature. Shiblī was not prepared to divest Islam completely of its "other-worldliness". Herein lies his only real difference with Sayyid Aḥmad Khān. He had not lost his transcendental touch, or his native style.

(3)

Once he had cast doubt on the certainty and finality of the basic tenet of nineteenth-century science and posited the possibility of what may be called, for want of a better name, a supernatural law of nature, he could have very well pitched Islam against general scientific reason also, and enjoyed almost unlimited scope for imaginative and intuitive speculation and reasoning. But Shiblī did neither of these two things. Having secured a "reasoned" place for the supernatural in Islam Shiblī showed himself a consistent and devout believer in science and nature. He would not, indeed he could not, disengage himself from the general frame of contemporary scientific or natural reason. He knew, like Sayyid Aḥmad Khān, that, in order to be made acceptable to a modern educated Muslim who had been exposed to this rationalism, Islam had to be shown to stand its test—as far as possible. This indeed should have gone without saying in so far as this was the *raison d'être* of his new venture in the field of *kalām*. But there was more to his adherence to science and reason.

The fact is that Shiblī was no less an admirer of nineteenth-century science and reason than Sayyid Aḥmad Khān was. He was enthusiastic about the scientific spirit of the West, particularly its experimental, inductive method of which he made use at different places to bolster up his arguments.[14] He even accepted, and traced back to Muslim sources, scientific notions such as those of gravity, the atom, the death and rebirth of biological cells, evolution, indestructibility of matter and last, but not least, the natural law of causation.[15] The last mentioned may seem paradoxical in view of what was said earlier on the subject. But that was a reservation Shiblī had to make in order to explain the supernatural element in Islam. Otherwise, he was a firm believer in the law of nature and vehemently condemned those who did not believe in it.[16]

It is true that he did not, like Sayyid Aḥmad Khān, go so far as to deny the supernatural in Islam in order to make it the religion of nature, a kind of deism fashionable among the scientific circles of the nineteenth-century West. But to Shiblī as well Islam was a natural religion in the sense of being in consonance with the tenets of reason

14. See, for instance, *Al-Ghazālī*, pp. 184 ff.
15. *Sawāniḥ*, pp. 219-24.
16. See below, pp. 22, 28, 38 f.

and, with the single exception already mentioned, also with the tenets of science or nature. Thus with Shiblī reason does not absolutely coincide with science, the former being slightly larger than the latter. It is science which is subsumed under reason and not *vice versa*. As with Sayyid Aḥmad Khān, science and reason still play the most important role in Shiblī's theological project, but the order is reversed. In his "natural religion" (*diyānah ṭabī'ah*), of which the idea he borrowed, through Farīd Wajdī, from certain European writers, reason is given the paramount role in judging the truth of religious beliefs.[17] In fact, Shiblī prefaces his actual presentation of Islamic tenets with a brief discourse showing that Islam is the only religion which religiously calls upon man to use his own reason and investigate nature. In this connection, he cites those verses of the Qur'ān which enjoin upon man to think intelligently and to study nature as the signs of God.[18] Shiblī then goes on to demonstrate that Islamic tenets conform to reason. And in so doing he falls back upon the medieval Muslim *kalām*.

(4)

In his attempt to show the conformity between Islamic beliefs and reason Shiblī turned to medieval Muslim *kalām* partly because of his historical per-

17. *Al-Kalām*, pp. 24 f.

18. Ibid., pp. 26-29.

spective and sense of continuity and partly because he thought that the issues of *kalām* on a purely theological level have not really changed. "That part of old *'ilm-i kalām* which is useless today," Shiblī writes, "was insufficient before also, and the part that was useful then is useful today also, and will so remain always, since the correctness and actuality of a thing does not alter with the passage of time."[19] Thus Shiblī was not ready to throw away the medieval *kalām* material altogether. He would rather reconstruct *'ilm-i kalām* "according to old principles and new taste".[20] We need not elaborate upon the "new taste," as the meaning is already clear by now. One must, however, add that it also included a "clear and simple style" so that the arguments should be easily comprehensible and appealing. The new style may be compared with the "old method" in which "complex premises, logical terms and very subtle concepts were used, as a result of which the opponent was intimidated and fell silent, but it failed to create a condition of belief and intuition."[21] The question that must be answered is: What did Shiblī mean by "old principle"? What part of medieval *kalām* did he consider useful then and useful now? And for what reason?

Before answering this question we should first find out what precisely were the issues of *kalām* in Shiblī's view. Shiblī views medieval *kalām* as

19. *'Ilm al-Kalām*, p. 4. 20. Ibid. 21. *Al-Kalām*, p. 6.

falling into two essentially different categories which he respectively calls traditional and rational: that which evolved out of the disputations between Islamic sects, and that which was developed to counter *falsafah*.[22] Shiblī concerns himself with the latter, "on whose pattern" he would reconstruct the new science of *kalām*.[23] Shiblī further subdivides the rational *kalām* into two parts: affirmation of Islamic beliefs and refutation of *falsafah*, *malāḥidah* and other religions.[24] At two different places he calls each of these two subdivisions, to the exclusion of the other, the essence of *'ilm i kalām*.[25]

In the first subdivision Shiblī includes the following as the legitimate concerns of *kalām*: affirmation of the Creator, of the Unity of God, of Prophecy, of the Qur'ān as the word of God and of the Hereafter. The rest he regards as irrelevant or inessential. He points out that hundreds of issues which either had nothing at all to do with Islam, negatively or positively, or at least had no essential relation with it, were included among the beliefs of Islam. A large part of the efforts expended in *'ilm-i kalām* was wasted in affirming these beliefs. Among the irrelevant he mentions issues such as whether the attributes of God are, or are not, identical with His essence, whether the Qur'ān is created or uncreated, whether actions

22. *'Ilm al-Kalām*, p. 9. 23. Ibid.
24. Ibid., p. 163; *Al-Ghazālī*, p. 168.
25. *'Ilm al-Kalām*, pp. 90, 196.

are part of faith or external to it, etc. Among the non-essentials he mentions those issues which resulted from trying to determine the nature or reality of the invisible world, namely, angelology and eschatology.[26] Although Shiblī took a stand on almost all the major issues of the first kind, he never took them up as a feature of his *kalām*.[27] He did devote, however, a full section to the discussion of issues of the second kind, even though he relegated them to a secondary position.[28]

Shiblī would have the second subdivision also drastically curtailed. Though he does not decry the medieval Muslim attempts to refute the religions other than Islam, the fact that he devotes only two and a half pages to describe them,[29] coupled with his subsequent lack of any marked interest in other religions (he mentions their beliefs only incidentally, without turning them into a matter of real dispute),[30] would indicate that he did not regard this line of *kalām* as important, at least not any more. Indeed, if the fact that he quotes al-Ghazālī to the effect that, except for those who rejected Islam after its reality

26. Ibid., pp. 196 f.; *Al-Kalām*, pp. 167-71. Also see *Makātīb*, I, 139.

27. For instance, the question of free-will and predestination in Islam: Shiblī felt very strongly about it, so much so that eventually he took it up in the *Sawāniḥ* (pp. 185-94; also see below, pp. 55 f.). But he does not consider it a legitimate concern of *kalām* and consequently does not include it in his *Al-Kalām*.

28. *Al-Kalām*, pp. 167-218.

29. *'Ilm al-Kalām*, pp. 163-65.

30. *Al-Kalām*, pp. 143-67.

had been fully explained to them, all non-Muslims are excusable and God will have mercy on them,[31] is an indication of the trend of Shiblī's own mind, he would rather make peace with other religions.

More interesting is Shiblī's view regarding the standpoint of *kalām vis-a-vis* the Greek *falsafah.* He says: "The *mutakallimīn* committed blunders [in their refutation of Greek *falsafah*]; the issues which they thought belonged to Greek *falsafah* did not really belong to it, and those which really belonged to it were more probably not against Islam."[32] Shiblī mentions, on the authority of al-Fārābī and Ibn Rushd, several views which were mistakenly attributed to the Greek philosophers; for instance, that Aristotle and Plato did not believe in reward and punishment, while in fact they did, that the *falāsifah* did not believe in miracles, and that their interpretation of *waḥy* and *ru'yā* was against Islamic belief, while in fact nothing is reported from them on the subject, etc.[33] Shiblī also lists those issues which did concern Greek *falsafah*, but were mistakenly regarded as being against Islam, for instance, the eternity of the world.[34] Thus, according to Shiblī, *falsafah* or Judaism or Christianity did not really pose a

31. *Al-Ghazālī*, pp. 291 f.

32. *'Ilm al-Kalām*, p. 90; in another place (p. 165): "apparently seemed against Islam"; in yet another place (p. 86): had "no concern" with Islam.

33. Ibid., pp. 166-70.

34. Ibid., pp. 170-73.

problem for the science of *kalām*.[35] Refutation of the *falsafah* should not indeed be regarded as proper *kalām*.[36]

The proper concern and real problem of *kalām* was the refutation of the atheists (*malāḥidah*) who did not believe in any religion and criticised every religion. Though they were against all the accepted beliefs of Islam, their main target was the Qur'ān in respect to its contents and style and thus its revealed or miraculous nature.[37] This singling out of *malāḥidah* as the number one enemy of Islam was in fact Shiblī's justification for going back to the medieval *kalām* in his quest for new *kalām* material. "It is surprising," he writes, "that, despite such progress of philosophy today and despite endless increase in the tendency towards shrewdness, fault-finding and scepticism, the objections being made on religious matters now-a-days are not superior in force, subtlety and number than those which the earlier *malāḥidah* made."[38] Thus, what Shiblī wated to do was to affirm the basic Islamic tenets over against the objections of the atheists with the help of the arguments used in the past. But the question still remains:

35. Ibid., p. 174.

36. Ibid., p. 166. He intended to write a separate monograph on medieval Muslim attempts at the refutation of *falsafah*—as an undertaking in the history of *falsafah* and not of *kalām*.

37. Ibid., pp. 174 ff. Shiblī wanted to write a separate volume, in his *kalām* series, on the Qur'ān entitled " 'Ulūm al-Qur'ān". *Al-Kalām*, p 1.

38. *'Ilm al-Kalām*, p. 175. See *Al-Kalām*, p. 40.

which part of the medieval *kalām* he regarded as useful for that purpose and what did he mean by the "old principles"? The answer lies in learning which of the various schools of *kalām* and which of the numerous *mutakallimīn* Shiblī preferred to the others and for what reasons.

Shiblī may or may not be a neo-Mu'tazilite modernist (or whatever that term means) like Sayyid Aḥmad Khān,[39] but he was deadly against Ash'arism. The Ash'arite *kalām* which had remained arrested and static for centuries and offered a method of argumentation which looked ridiculously unreasonable, especially against the nineteenth-century rationalist background, was not acceptable to him at all. In a sense, Shiblī's works on *kalām* are nothing but a concerted attempt to discredit the basic tenets of Ash'arism, and uphold those of Mu'tazilism. In fact, as we shall see later, his interest in rationalism did not even stop with the Mu'tazilites, but, in several instances, led him to welcome ideas from philosophers and mystics. The beliefs peculiar to the Ash'arites have

39. Aziz Ahmad, op. cit., p. 83. One really fails to understand what Aziz Ahmad precisely means by the term neo-Mu'tazilite modernist and why would he want to characterise Shiblī so very differently from Sayyid Aḥmad Khān in this respect. If neo-Mu'tazilite modernism means the adoption of the nineteenth-century natural philosophy lock, stock and barrel, then he is probably right in not regarding Shiblī a neo-Mu'tazilite modernist. But if it means adoption of a generally rationalist outlook and scientific worldview, and rejection of Ash'arism, then Shiblī ought to be classified along with Sayyid Aḥmad Khān.

an appeal, according to Shiblī, only to a simple, unquestioning mind in contradistinction to a philosophic, questioning mind which is attracted towards the Mu'tazilite beliefs.[40] The significance of the Ash'arite beliefs, in Shiblī's eyes, is merely historical: they are the outcome of the first attempt in Muslim theology by Abū al-Ḥasan al-Ash'arī to strike a middle course between reason and tradition. Unfortunaley, this attempt ended up by being against reason, as is evident in al-Ash'arī's attempt to prove the vision of God and miracles.[41] Yet, with the advent of *mutakallimīn* like al-Ghazālī there was hope that the defects of Ash'arism would be removed and that it would attain perfection. The Mongol invasion, however, cut its intellectual development short—though unfortunately not its spread.[42] Shiblī criticises the characteristic Ash'arite doctrines in these words: "You can judge for yourself who can ever prove such things as that God encumbers with a responsibility which is beyond human capacity (*taklīf mā lā yuṭāq*), that effects are not related to causes, that body is not the condition of life, that man turns into a donkey by magic."[43] At another place, criticising the argument of the "superficial Ash'arites" (*Ashā'irah-i ẓāhirīyyīn*) in support of the external existence of the invisible

40. *'Ilm al-Kalām*, pp. 11 f.
41. Ibid., pp. 63 f.
42. Ibid., p. 84, and the preceding pages; also p. 161.
43. Ibid., p. 87.

world, Shiblī says: "It is these childish argumentations and unbounded speculations (*iḥtimālāt*) which have made all the people believe in magic and scores of far-fetched things."[44] Even in the affirmation of the beliefs proper to Islam, such as the existence and Unity of God, Prophecy and the Hereafter, Shiblī is in almost total disagreement with the usual Ash'arite method of argumentation, as will become evident later.

Shiblī's attraction towards Mu'tazilities' characteristic doctrines must already be evident from his rejection of the parallel Ash'arite doctrines in particular, and Ash'arite methodology in general. However, in view of its unaccustomed nature it seems necessary to document the fact. To begin with, in connection with the political origin of the theological discussions under the Umayyads, Shiblī mentions favourably the stand taken by Ma'bad, Ghaylān and Jahm on the question of free-will and predestination.[45] This inclination becomes still more clear where Shiblī mentions the Ash'arite and Mu'tazilite beliefs resulting from their respective stands on the question of reason versus tradition. Characterising this question as the real basis of difference between the Ash'arites and the Mu'tazilites, he declares that it is at this point where the boundaries of the *arbāb-i ẓāhir* (meaning the Ash'arites) and *ahl-i naẓar* (meaning

44. *Al-Kalām*, p. 198.

45. *'Ilm al-Kalām*, pp. 17-19.

the Mu'tazilites) become totally apart.[46] Though he disapproves their intolerant attitude under al-Māmūn, he mentions with pride that the Mu'tazilites were mostly Ḥanafites (he was a devoted Ḥanafite himself) and also gives a list of early *muḥaddithīn* who were regarded by al-Dhahabī and Ibn Ḥajar as Qadarites or Mu'tazilites.[47]

Thus, Shiblī's sympathy for, and agreement with, the Mu'tazilites was unmistakable. The major issues on which he took up the same views as the Mu'tazilites are: God's commands are always based on reason, justice and goodness; things are possessed of inalienable properties both in moral and physical sense, and there is in operation an unbroken chain of cause and effect in this world; and, finally, man has freedom of will and action. One need hardly re-emphasise the point how necessary it was for Shiblī to uphold these views if he wanted to show the reasonableness of Islam in the nineteenth- and early twentieth-century humanistic world dominated by natural rationalism.

The elaborations made above regarding Shiblī's pro-Mu'tazilite stance provide us then with part of the answer to our original question as to what Shiblī meant by "old principles" and what he regarded as "useful" in the medieval *kalām*. Part of the answer seems to be indicated by Shiblī's appealing to the ideas of Muslim philosophers and

46. Ibid., pp. 22 f.

47. Ibid., pp. 25, 28-30.

mystics or rather philosopher-mytics. The Mu'tazilites were indeed very useful and welcome in so far as they helped counter the absolutely unreasonable and unscientific and God-centred attitude of the Ash'arites and helped to present a reasonable, scientific and man-centred picture of Islam. They were not of much help, however, in explaining the supernatural or invisible elements in Islam. Although they tended towards a spiritual interpretation of the supernatural, they did not go all the way,[48] as the philosophers did. Like the Ash'arites, they also failed to fully amalgamate reason and tradition in Islam, or to achieve a rationalised Islam suitable to Shiblī's liking and purpose.

It, was, therefore, to the philosophers that Shiblī turned next in his quest for reason, and thus for respectability and acceptability in Islam. He admits the incongruity of this move, but devotes a full section to the *ḥukamā'-i Islām* in his history of *kalām* He is well aware that *mutakallimīn* and *ḥukamā'* are generally known to be in opposition to each other, but believes that the opposition is not real. "No doubt the general term *ḥukamā'* can be put in contraposition to the title *mutakallimīn*," he writes, "but when it is qualified by *Islām*, the veil of alienation is lifted; Imām Ghazālī and Ibn Rushd, who are called *ḥukamā'-i Islām*, are also in the vanguard

48. *Al-Kalām*, p. 187.

of *'ilm-i kalām.*"[49] If another proof of their interrelation, in fact a further justification for making use of philosophy in theology, is needed, Shiblī provides it on the authority of Ibn Taymīyyah and Ibn Rushd. According to them, al-Fārābī and Ibn Sīnā adopted their characteristic Islamic theological doctrines, not from the Greeks whose theology was imperfect, but from the early theologians of Islam (*qudamā'-i mutakallimīn*) themselves.[50] In varying details, Shiblī abstracts the ideas of al-Fārābī, Ibn Sīnā, Ibn Miskawayh and Shaykh al-Ishrāq (he has already dealt with Ibn Rushd among the *mutakallimīn* and with al-Ghazālī in a separate monograph) on such issues as Soul, Prophecy, Angels, Revelation and Miracles.[51] The thing which appeals to Shiblī most about these Muslim philosophers and which he stresses again and again is of course that their "main aim is conformity between *falsafah* and *sharī'ah.*"[52] That is what prompted him to own even the notorious *Ikhwān al-Ṣafā'*,[53] and write sarcastically that Shaykh al-Ishrāq "mentions Zoroaster and others as Prophets, and counts the Greek philosophers among the ones close to God; what more

49. *'Ilm al-Kalām*, p. 120.

50. Ibid., pp. 153-56. It is not quite clear what exactly does Shiblī mean by *qudamā'-i mutakallimīn*. Probably it was just another way of referring to the early Mu'tazilites such as Abū al-Hudhayl, Hishām b. al-Ḥakam, Naẓẓām, and others. Also see *Al-Kalām*, p. 2.

51. *'Ilm al-Kalām*, pp 121-53.

52. Ibid., pp. 121; also see pp. 123 f., 125, 145, 146 f.

53. Ibid., pp. 145 f.

evidence is required for [Shaykh al-Ishrāq's] ***kufr***!"[54]

Now we come somewhat closer to knowing what Shiblī really meant when he talked, in connection with the formulation of a new ***'ilm-i kalām***, of the old principles and the still useful part of the medieval ***kalām***. He had in mind essentially the doctrines of the Mu'tazilites and the Muslim philosophers. That, however, is not the end of the matter. Shiblī was aware that in referring back to the doctrines of the Mu'tazilites and Muslim philosophers he was face to face with two great difficulties, one practical and the other strategic. The practical difficulty was that not a single work of the Mu'tazilites, those "ancients" of ***'ilm-i kalām***, was extant; all that he had available were quotations from their works and references to their doctrines in later, mostly Ash'arite, works on sects and theology, and specifically in the great exegetical work of al-Rāzī.[55] The strategic difficulty that Shiblī faced was that if he was writing for the benefit of the contemporary Muslim readership, he could hardly expect to have the doctrines of Mu'tazilites and Muslim philosophers—both considered heretics by most Muslims—accepted on their own authority. In order to have receptive ears, in any number, for his words he had to find respectable mouthpieces of Ash'arite denomination, who had

54. Ibid., p. 149; also see pp. 145-53.
55. *Al-Kalām*, p. 2; *'Ilm al-Kalām*, p. 162.

either absorbed those doctrines in the recesses of their thoughts or at least had a kind word or two to say about them. Theologians like al-Ghazālī and al-Rāzī, who could talk through both sides of their mouths, were as if made to measure for this purpose.[56] This should not lead one to conclude that Shiblī was merely using such persons. On the contrary, he truly believed in them, especially in al-Ghazālī whom he regarded as a thinker too independent to be really bound by the absurd, traditional Ash'arite system, and perhaps also too creative not to have contributed something on his own. In fact, before Rūmī finally caught his eye and won his heart, Shiblī was almost hypnotised by al-Ghazālī, so much so that he once wrote: "If the edifice of the new *'ilm-i kalām* can be erected today, it can be erected on the basis of his ideas."[57] But the fact remains that what attracted Shiblī in al-Ghazālī and al-Rāzī was not the fact that they were Ash'arites—the usefulness of this fact apart, Shiblī never compromised his position *vis-a vis* Ash'arism itself—but that they were inconsistent Ash'arites; that despite their professed, public Ash'arism, in some crucial respects they surreptitiously went in for Mu'tazilism and Islamic *falsafah*, in short, for

56. He was still accused of being infatuated with Mu'tazilism, and his disciple-biographer had to apologise for him by saying that it was actually the love of Māturīdism. Sayyid Sulaymān Nadwī, op. cit., p. 829.

57. *'Ilm al-Kalām*, p. 146.

reason. Al-Ghazālī, indeed, "completely merged *manqūl* with *ma'qūl*, and with such finesse that neither of them suffered in the process."[58] It is that accomplishment which makes him so great in the eyes of Shiblī.

Shiblī has taken many pains and pages in showing from the horse's own mouth the duality in al-Ghazālī's theological thought and works. Al-Ghazālī upheld Ash'arism and wrote one book after another in support of it, but he believed that "Ash'arism is good for the common people; otherwise, it neither contains the reality, nor can it give real satisfaction." Consequently, he produced another series of books (such as *Jawāhir al-Qur'ān*, *Munqidh min al Ḍalāl*, *Maḍnūn Ṣaghīr wa Kabīr*, *Ma'ārij al-Quds*, *Mishkāt al-Anwār*) in which, instead of following the Ash'arite pattern, he disclosed the hidden "realities". But he would not have those books generally published for fear of ununderstanding commoners and *'ulamā'*.[59] Not heeding such counsels, however, Shiblī considers it incumbent upon the authors of the new *'ilm-i kalām* to throw these secret treasures open to the public. That is precisely what he would want to do himself.[60]

These "realities" are nothing but the doctrines of the Mu'tazilites and the Muslim philosophers.

58. Ibid.

59. Ibid., pp. 65 f., 146 f., 161 f.; *Al-Kalām*, pp. 2-6 ; *Al-Ghazālī*, pp 189-201.

60. *Al-Kalām*, p. 6.

Al-Ghazālī, according be Shiblī, rejected the characteristic Ash'arite doctrines such as that there is no causal chain and no inalienable property or nature, that things are not good and bad in themselves, that there is no reason, order or system in the creation of the world, in favour of the corresponding Mu'tazilite doctrines.[61] Even in the case of legitimately Islamic doctrines—particularly Prophecy, miracles, soul, life after death, reward and punishment—he gave up the Ash'arite method and brought forward new arguments, some of which were in use among the *ḥukamā'*. Indeed, on the questions of soul, supernatural events and punishment in the Hereafter he followed Ibn Sīnā; and on the questions of revelation, and visions and hearings of the Prophets he copied Ibn Miskawayh.[62] The next major contribution of al-Ghazālī to *kalām*—besides the introduction and employment of *falsafah*, and adoption of Mu'tazilism in some of the crucial issues (though the latter fact faded into oblivion under his blatant, public Ash'arism)—was, according to Shiblī, the distinction between the essential and inessential beliefs in Islam and, in addition, regulation of the principles of *ta'wīl* of *nuṣūṣ shar'īyyah* which, on the one hand, discouraged the practice of *takfīr* and brought greater harmony among the sects

61. *Al-Ghazālī*, pp. 209-13, 296 f., 362 f.

62. Ibid., pp. ?24-64 (particularly 224, 242, 252, 256); also pp. 297-300, 356-62; *'Ilm al-Kalām*, pp. 144 f.

and, on the other hand, opened the way to further rationalisation.[63] Shiblī is very appreciative of these contributions and makes use of them in his new *kalām*.

Al-Rāzī, apparently the most aggressive Ash'arite of all times,[64] also held, according to Shiblī, actually quite different views which he expressed mostly in his *Tafsīr* through the tongue of those whom he collectively calls at different places *ḥukamā'-i Islām* or *arbāb-i ma'qūlāt*.[65] Shiblī is particularly appreciative of al-Rāzī's *Tafsīr* in so far as it is written on "rationalistic" lines, and says that al-Rāzī

> "has been much more free and unprejudiced in the *Tafsīr* than in his works on *kalām*; frequently . . . quotes the opinions of *ḥukamā'-i Islām* and, though they are against the Ash'arites, praises them and approves them; moreover, he makes use of the *tafsīrs* of his antagonists, the Mu'tazilites, often mentioning their doctrines without any criticism; in fact sometimes praising them involuntarily."

Shiblī appreciatively mentions several such "real views of the *imām* which are the core of the science of *kalām*" from the *Tafsīr*. What makes them the core of the science of *kalām* is of course that they are "in accordance with *falsafah* and *'aql*". Likewise, Shiblī quotes from the *Tafsīr* instances of al-Rāzī's preference for the interpretations made

63. *Al-Ghazālī*, pp. 213-23, 285-93 ; *'Ilm al-Kalām*, pp. 190-96 ; *al-Kalām*, pp. 173-97.

64. *'Ilm al-Kalām*, p. 72.

65. Ibid., pp. 73-76, 120 f.

by the Mu'tazilite exegist Abū Muslim Iṣfahānī.[66] Shiblī is also very pleased with al-Rāzī for having refuted the "anti-rational" Jewish traditions of *tafsīr* literature, something which the Mu'tazilites also did but could not get away with simply because they were Mu'tazilites.[67] Shiblī, however, is aware of the fact that the *manqūl* still outbalances the *ma'qūl* in al-Rāzī and that he wrote books in refutation of Mu'tazilism. He, therefore, quotes, as a further proof of his real, rationlist views which he could not present openly for fear of persecution, adverse comments on al-Rāzī's beliefs by traditionists like al-Dhahabī and Ibn Ḥajar to the effect that he "created doubts about the fundamentals of religion" and that he "presented the objections of the opponents more forcefully than the reply on behalf of the *Ahl al-Sunnah.*"[68] Shiblī singles out al-Rāzī's alternate argument on Prophecy in his last work, *Maṭālib-i 'Āliyah,* to be appended (along with al-Ghazālī's argument on the same subject from *Ma'ārij al-Quds*) to his *Al-Kalām,* perhaps because the later writers had deliberately ignored it on account of its being out of step with the Ash'arite doctrines.[69]

Al-Ghazālī and al-Rāzī were by no means the only pillars of Shiblī's new *kalām,* or the only bridges to the good old principles and to the use-

66. Ibid., pp. 74-76, 77, 178-83.
67. Ibid., pp. 78 f.
68. Ibid., pp. 79-81.
69. Ibid., p. 204; *Al-Kalām,* pp. 224-59.

ful in medievel *kalām*, even if thev were the ones who, for reasons made obvious, were played up the most. The only other person to compete with them in this respect was the relatively late Shāh Walī Allāh, partly for the same reasons but partly also, as in the case of al-Ghazālī, because of his own contribution to *kalām*. There were other, earlier *mutakallimīn*, not so prominent and seldom referred to in the presentation of the actual content of the new *kalām*, but very useful in demolishing the edifice of Ash'arism and building up a case for a greater and greater role of reason in Islamic theology, Shiblī's one and only obsession. No other consideration weighed more with him in the selection of a thinker or selection from his ideas than his rationalism. That was one qualification which they all, persons as diverse an Ibn Taymīyyah and Ibn Rushd, had in common, at least in the eyes of Shiblī. Besides harmonising reason and tradition and severely criticising the Ash'arite *kalām* for being neither rational nor traditional, Ibn Rushd made an original contribution to the science of *kalām* in that he claimed and demonstrated that Qur'ānic argumentation on theological matters is not merely rhetorical and persuasive but logical and demonstrative. Shiblī was attracted by this argument and made use of it in his new *kalām*.[70] Ibn Taymīyyah has to his credit perhaps the boldest criticism so far

70. *'Ilm al-Kalām*, pp. 96-99.

of the Ash'arite doctrines such as that everything that exists can be perceived by the senses, all bodies are alike and are composed of atoms, God did not create anything with a reason, nor did He characterise bodies with faculties and natures, and there are not underlying reasons in His law. Despite being "bigoted, crusty and intensely inimical to philosophy," he preferred the doctrines of the natural and mathematical sciences over those of the *mutakallimīn*, and also held that the reality of the events after death is different from what is given to understand.[71]

During his intellectual journey from al-Ghazālī to Rūmī the only person who really excited Shiblī and left a lasting impression on his mind was Shāh Walī Allāh, or rather his *Ḥujjat Allāh al-Bālighah* which Shiblī regards as a work of *kalām* since it treats the *sharī'ah*—and not merely *'aqā'id* in the usual, narrow sense—as if it were the subject-matter of *kalām*, and shows the revealed nature of the *sharī'ah* through its miraculous perfection. Shāh Walī Allāh was of course going to show that "all the matters of the *sharī'ah* are in accordance with reason"; and he was also "generally against the characteristic doctrines of the Ash'arites". But Shiblī is particularly enthusiastic about two things. One is Shāh Walī Allāh's concept of non-elemental or non-material worlds (*'ālam-i mithāl, 'ālam-i barzakh*) which, if

71. Ibid., pp. 102, 106 f., 184.

only the '*ulamā*' would also accept it, Shiblī regards as the peacemaker between philosophy and religion since it accommodates all the supernatural elements in Islam in the way philosophers would have it. The other thing which thrills Shiblī in Shāh Walī Allāh is the novel way he goes about underlining the miraculousness of the Qur'ān through the contents of its teaching on ethics, purification of the soul, Unity of God, Prophecy and the Hereafter. Shiblī was also impressed with Shāh Walī Allāh's explanation of the repetition and disorderliness in the Qur'ān, something which had upset Carlyle.[72]

With these men and their ideas at his command Shiblī turned to writing his theology for today. We have already noticed how Shiblī was acting under modern influences in the choice of his men and their ideas, not to mention the fact that the very rationale of his theological enterprise was provided by the modern rationalist impulse. He did not become a modernist because he was impressed by the spirit and thinking of the Mu'tazilites and the Muslim philosophers. He went and got himself impressed by their spirit and thinking because he was a modernist with an intense sense of his Islamic past, because he wanted to be a modernist within his own historico-religious tradition, in short, because he wanted to internalise an external impulse. At the same time he was

72. Ibid., pp. 111-19; *Al-Kalam*, pp. 201-09.

prudent enough, perhaps learning from Sayyid Aḥmad Khān's fiasco, not to go courting medieval Islamic rationalists too openly. We shall now have the opportunity to see this under-cover, medievalised modernism at work in the actual layout of Shiblī's new *kalām*.

We also noted above that Shiblī, who had set out with the purpose of offering a solution different from that of Sayyid Aḥmad Khān, was apparently able to depart from the latter rather crucially. Failing to fully maintain that science and religion operated at two different levels or in two different spheres, Shiblī challenged, even if at the cost of confusion in terms, Sayyid Aḥmad Khān's interpretation of nature as a closed system of immutable laws which allowed of no supernatual intervention. We shall be seeing again this departure from Sayyid Aḥmad Khān's stand, for whatever worth it is, in Shiblī's actual restatement of Islamic faith for modern times. But often enough Shiblī will be found agreeing rather than disagreeing with Sayyid Aḥmad Khān's solution concerning the specific religious beliefs of Islam, perhaps because he was drawing upon more or less the same sources as Sayyid Aḥmad Khān did.

(5)

The problem of the existence of God was obviously not stirring enough for Shiblī—perhaps because he felt that the belief in His existence is not really consequent upon rational arguments—for he dealt with it in a rather hurried and cursory manner, without his usual verve and relish. He starts by rejecting the old arguments from the contingency and movement of the world, because they depend on positing the absurdity of infinite regress to which Shiblī does not subscribe. The former is all the more unacceptable to him because it further depends on the assumption, unsupported by experience, that matter itself is contingent. These arguments have the added weakness, according to Shiblī, that they affirm only a cause of the causes and not necessarily an efficient and powerful God[73] (noticeable here is the difference from Sayyid Aḥmad Khān for whom God is the "First Cause," in the emanationist spirit of the Muslim philosophers).[74] For his part Shiblī, besides asserting that belief in God is part of human nature (Max Müller and others are cited), prefers the Qur'ānic argument from harmony in the universe (again citing the European *ḥukamā'*, such as Newton and Spencer) as an aid to the innate belief.[75]

Shiblī is well aware of the atheists' (*malāḥidah's*) arguments against the existence of God and describes them in detail.[76] But it seems that, like his medieval predecessors, he presented the arguments of his opponents too forcefully to be

73. Ibid., pp. 30-34.
74. Fazlur Rahman, *Islam*, p. 218.
75. *Al-Kalām*, pp. 35-39.
76. Ibid., pp. 40-54.

able really to counter them.[77] For instance, he had to admit that in the absence of positive evidence on the existence or non-existence of a thing we tend, in daily experience, to deny its existence. Shiblī, however, would not admit its implications for the exitence of God, without explaining himself.[78] Likewise, he responds to their arguments by readily, indeed eagerly, admitting with them that the world, composed of atoms, is eternal (a doctrine held, according to Shiblī, by the Mu'tazilites[79] and by Muslim philosophers such as al-Fārābī, Ibn Sīnā and Ibn Rushd; indeed, he says, as Ibn Rushd has pointed out, the doctrine is indicated by the Qur'ān itself); that the motion of atoms is essential to matter; that there are various laws of nature in accordance with which these atoms meet and coalesce so that faculties and properties are born into them. Shiblī stops short, however, of following the immediate inference that the world can be imagined without a Creator, and insists that it does not solve the problem. There must be a superior power which controls and harmonises the innumerable laws of nature, since harmony is not an essential property of these laws. (Milane Edward and others are cited.)[80]

77. Cf. Sayyid Sulaymān Nadwī, op. cit., pp. 831 f.
78. *Al-Kalām*, pp 41 f.
79. He is mistaken in attributing this doctrine to the Mu'tazilites.
80. *Al-Kalām*, pp. 54-57.

Obviously, Shiblī is struggling to reconcile the idea of an eternal world with the idea of an eternal God. He must have felt that once one of these propositions is affirmed the other is rendered superfluous. But he could not let go of the idea of God for obvious reasons, and would not let go of the idea of an eternal world because to him it was an established scientific truth proven by the indestructibility of matter. Had he thought that the eternity of the world was merely a medieval dogma of theologians or philosophers, he would have gladly thrown it out of the window.[81]

To prove the Unity of God Shiblī employs the argument of the absurdity of two complete causes of a single effect, which again he bases on the Qur'ān. He also emphasises the fact that the idea of the Unity of God is universal to all religions, Islam's uniqueness consisting in the perfection of the idea. Perfect Unity of God is also needed, according to him, for the spiritual and moral well-being of humans.[82]

Shiblī rejects the argument based on biological evolution and the fact of evil in the world against the existence of a God attributed with power, wisdom, will, justice and mercy. He maintains that evolution, properly understood, is an argument in favour of His power. He argues also that

81. Eventually he had to throw it out of the window when he found himself faced with the *fatwā* of heresy : Sayyid Sulaymān Nadwī, op. cit., p. 823.

82. *Al-Kalām*, pp. 59-62.

it was not possible to create good without also necessarily creating evil; the apparent flourishing of evil, moreover, should not be judged on the basis of such a short span of life in this world.[83]

(6)

When it comes to the question of Prophecy, Shiblī appears to be at home. He is in obvious disagreement with the usual Ash'arite notion that Prophecy is an office which God bestows arbitrarily upon whomsoever He wishes and that miracle is a necessary condition for Prophecy distinguishing a true *nabī* from a false one.[84]

He takes up the latter part of the question first. To begin with, he does not believe that miracles can or ever have occurred in a way so as to break the natural law of causation. However, because of their unusual quality or their deviation from a generally prevalent pattern (*'ām 'ādat-i jāriyah*) miracles may look as though they contravene nature. In reality there are always natural reasons for miraculous happenings, even if they are extraordinary. He cites Ibn Sīnā and Shāh Walī Allāh in his support; and takes al-Rāzī to book for trying to prove the possibility of interruption in natural behaviour by "some unusual spherical movement," saying that he did not realise that in such a case it was no longer an interruption in natural behaviour. Thus as long as an event does

83. Ibid., pp. 57-59.

84. Ibid., p. 62.

not violate the natural law of cause and effect, but only deviates from the *'ādah*, that is to say, contradicts what is generally believed to be natural at a given point in time and space, Shiblī does not deny the possibility and occurrence of miracles.[85] And this marks Shiblī's major departure from Sayyid Aḥmad Khān who on principle rejects the possibility of miracles, perhaps because, being more thoroughly consistent, he does not make the illegitimate distinction between *'ādah* and natural law.

Indeed, in a section devoted especially to this question Shiblī takes the "modern group" (*firqah-i jadīdah*; the reference is obviously to Sayyid Aḥmad Khān) to task for going to the other extreme, in contraposition to the "credulous Muslims," by denying the occurrence of an event if it is in appearance contrary to nature, and by indulging in *ta'wīl* of the Qur'ān on such occasions. But, Shiblī says:

> "*kharq-i 'ādah* is a necessary element of all religions, and it cannot be denied that in Islam too there is some trace of it . . . no doubt, the Ash'arite excess in this matter has gone to the extent of childish superstition, but total denial [of miracles] is also nothing short of obstinacy."

Raising the questions: Have all the laws of nature been determined? Can we be rest assured that the things which we are taking to be the laws of nature

85. Ibid., pp. 77-84.

are really so?—Shiblī answers that "the investigations and experiments of modern sciences have discovered hundreds of laws of nature which were totally unknown before, and this process continues." Things which were regarded as impossible, Shiblī says, are being proven to be possible.[86] In this connection he points out the results of experiments in mesmerism and spiritusalism.[87] Thus, he says:

"No intelligent person can deny the *khawāriq-i 'ādāt*, but the difference is that superstitious and credulous people believe that they happen directly by the *qudrah* of God, and the elite (like al-Ghazālī, Ibn Rushd, Shah Walī Allāh and Ibn Sīnā) believe that since everything in this world is bound up with causes, therefore, there is one reason or another for these *kharq-i 'ādāt*."[88]

Indeed, Shiblī suggests on the authority of Ibn Sīnā and al-Ghazālī that the miracles of the Prophets occur due to their developed psychic powers.[89]

But Shiblī was reluctant about accepting that a specific miracle had actually occurred. Even in the case of the Qur'ān, unless the text is conclusive (*qaṭ'ī al-dalālah*), he would not (like Qaffāl, Abū Muslim Iṣfahānī and Abū Bakr Aṣamm) take it as referring to a miracle, not to speak of "all kinds of absurd and really impossible things" affirmed by the Ash'arites and the generality of Muslims.[90]

86. Ibid., pp. 115 f.
87. Ibid., pp. 117-26.
88. Ibid., p. 126.
89. Ibid., pp. 128 f.
90. Ibid., pp. 129 f.

He was especially angry with the Ash'arites for stretching the bounds of possibility to include all kinds of improbabilities, while not realising the more immediate likelihood that the narrator of the event may have been mistaken.[91] It is remarkable that, despite his basic divergence from Sayyid Aḥmad Khān's approach and aim in the matter, Shiblī shows close affinity with him in practically discouraging belief in superstitions and miracles and encouraging belief in an essentially scientific *weltanschauung*.

To come back to the question of Prophecy, although Shiblī admits, with qualification, the possibility and occurrence of miracles, he still would not regard them as a proof of Prophecy. On this matter one should take Shiblī's zestful exposition of al-Rāzī's hypothetical objection to the Ash'arite position as well as Ibn Rushd's objection to the same, as representing his own views. Both of these objections may be reduced to the same basic argument: there is no way to know the *kharq-i 'ādah* of a true Prophet even if the event really were an effect without a cause or a cause without an effect, from that of a pretender who may be a *jinn*, a devil or a magician capable, according to the Ash'arites, of *kharq-i 'ādah*. Shiblī would also hold that one cannot tell an instance of prophetic *kharq-i 'ādah* from a trick or a psychic effect of a non-prophet.[92]

91. Ibid., p. 83.

92. Ibid., pp. 67-73.

Not only can miracle not be offered as a proof of Prophecy, but in Shiblī's view (based mainly on Qur'ānic verses but also on statements by al-Rāzī, Shāh Walī Allāh and Ibn Rushd) it has no essential relationship with Prophecy.[93] The fact that he can turn a stick into a snake, Shiblī says, following al-Rāzī's hypothetical objector, has nothing to do with the Prophet's ability to lead people to happiness in the two worlds, any more than the ability to endure hunger for twenty consecutive days will make one an expert in geometry.[94] Shiblī is fond of quoting a statement of al-Ghazālī saying: " . . . hence, seek belief in Prophecy through this method and not through the turning of a stick into a snake or the splitting of the moon."[95] It is this "other method" which is the object of Shiblī's positive concern in the question of Prophecy—a method preferred by the *muḥaqqiqīn.*

This method is to know the reality of Prophecy and its function in human life and, then, to see whether the Prophet's teachings and his role are consistent with this reality and function. Shiblī quotes al-Rāzī, Shāh Walī Allāh, al-Ghazālī and Ibn Ḥazm at length to elaborate his point. The idea is that just as man has many other faculties or powers (*quwwaten*) he has been endowed with a spiritual power (*quwwat i qudsīyah yā malikah-i nubuwwah*) to perceive the ultimate realities and

93. Ibid , pp. 84-88.
94. Ibid., pp. 71 f.
95. Ibid., pp. 88, 89, 104.

moral concepts, for the compelling purposes of social organisation. This power, however, like the others, is distributed unequally among men, so much so that some are almost devoid of it. It is, therefore, a rational-natural necessity, at least it is not unlikely, that there be persons who have this power to the limit of perfection. Thus, they may also take care of others, less endowed, by standardising the law of morality and purifying the souls. These persons are Prophets; and this power at its perfection is not something acquired through intellectual processes. It is beyond the realm of intellect and learning. It is inborn. Prophets can be likened to the geniuses in other fields of human activity. Prophets are in a sense spiritual and moral geniuses. It is this genius or perceptive power which is called *ilhām* or *waḥy*, and which operates as natural instinct in lower forms of life.[96] (On comparison it will be found that Shiblī's views are akin to those of Sayyid Aḥmad Khān on the subject of the reality of revelation and Prophecy.)[97] One may incidentally, but significantly, observe here that, although Shiblī is not, unlike Sayyid Aḥmad Khān, in pursuit of a natural religion, he shows a tendency towards a human religion. Following his medieval masters, but perhaps inspired by modern humanism, he appears to be turning the God-man relationship into a man-God relationship. It seeems that in his

96. Ibid., pp. 89-102. 97. Aziz Ahmad, op. cit., pp. 43 f.

understanding it is man who reaches out to God rather than God to man. It is man who is the centre of religious activity rather than God.

Once it is recognised what Prophecy is, one cannot but know a Prophet, just as knowledge of *fiqh* brings recognition that al-Shāfi'ī was a *faqīh.* It is not only the teachings, especially the Qur'ān, but also the character of the Prophet which tell us that he is a true Prophet.[98] Such was Shiblī's method to prove the truthfulness of the Prophet. He wrote many pages to show the excellence of Islamic teachings and prefaced the exposition with a general discussion of the principles of the Prophets' method of teachings mainly derived from Shāh Walī Allāh. In that preface he tried to make two or three points. Since the guidance of the common people is the paramount object of a Prophet's teachings, their level of understanding has been taken into consideration in the *sharī'ah* (the Qur'ān included). One should not, however, judge the *sharī'ah* on that basis alone, since it also contains pointers to the reality of things for the elite. It should not be judged on the basis of its extra-individual-spiritual and social-moral content either, since there the contemporary level of scientific and historical knowledge has been taken into account. Finally, even in the proper concerns of the *sharī'ah* one should not forget that the *sharī'ahs* prior to the Prophet's in general, and the Prophet's

98. *Al-Kalām*, pp. 103-05.

sharī'ah in particular, incorporated many local customs and practices which are now open to change.[99] With these preliminary remarks, Shiblī goes on to underline, in some detail, the excellence of the Prophet's teachings on theology, ethics, social code and the principles of civilisation as a proof of his Prophecy.[100]

After emphasising that Islam discouraged *taqlīd* in matters of belief (which later led to the Lutheran Reformation),[101] he points out the highly non-material concept of God in Islam (which astonished even Gibbon),[102] the direct relationship between man and God[103] and humanliness of the Prophet.[104] Allowing that the usual concept of reward and punishment in the Hereafter was good for the common people and that Islam employed it for that reason, Shiblī maintains that Islam is unique in indicating, at the same time, its reality (which bears close resemblance with Sayyid Aḥmad's view of it). As al-Ghazālī put it, reward and punishment are the inalienable effects of good and bad deeds on the soul. "Hell is right inside you," al-Ghazālī writes in his commentary on a Qur'ānic verse. Fondly quoting this and other commentaries by al-Ghazālī to the same effect, Shiblī tops them with this concluding remark from him: "If you

99. Ibid., pp. 105-15; also see below, pp. 70-73.
100. *Al-Kalām*, pp. 130-33.
101. Ibid., pp. 133-35.
102. Ibid., pp. 135-37.
103. Ibid., p. 137.
104. Ibid., pp. 137-39.

did not understand the meanings in this manner, then you did not get from the Qur'ān anything except the crust, as the cattle get only the husk from the wheat."[105] Next, Shiblī deals with rituals, human rights, the position of the women, the law of inheritance and the status of non-Muslims in a manner which has now become standard in the modern apologetics of Islam.[106]

(7)

Although Shiblī would rather have Islamic theology based only on the Unity of God and Prophethood of Muḥammad (peace of Allah be upon him), and tried even to belittle the rest of the dogmatic paraphernalia, he could not very well ignore these other doctrines, at least not those bearing upon the spiritual or invisible world, in other words, angelology and eschatology. These doctrines were the supernatural element of Islam *par excellence* and thus the most sensitive and vulnerable part of Islamic theology and for that matter perhaps of any theology. Shiblī was perfectly aware of their importance and he, therefore, dealt with them at some length. It is here indeed that one finds Shiblī fully and finally exposed. The mere fact that he gives the invisible world the alternative name of *ruḥānīyāt* should be a sufficient indication of the drift of his mind.[107] But he

105. Ibid., pp. 139-43; Aziz Ahmad, op. cit., p. 46.
106. *Al-Kalām*, pp. 143-67.
107. Ibid., pp. 167-71.

makes his intent abundantly clear in the course of the actual discussion which he prefaces by a long discourse on *ta'wīl* derived from al-Ghazālī.

Mentioning the three historic positions—i.e. literal, metaphoric and spiritual interpretations—taken on the question of the reality of invisible matters or *mutashābihāt* in Islam, Shiblī regards the defining of the scope of *ta'wīl* (which increases gradually with the literalists, the common Ash'arites, Māturīdites, Mu'tazilites and *ḥukamā'*) as pertinent to this question, and to this end he quotes al-Ghazālī extensively. We need not go into the matter except to point out that Shiblī, though very appreciative of al-Ghazālī's elaborations of the principles of *ta'wīl* as well of his actual *ta'wīl* in a number of matters, differs from him on a fundamental point Al-Ghazālī is against employing *ta'wīl* in matters eschatological on the basis of the principle that they are not rationally impossible. Shiblī would not permit this stand to go unchallenged. First, he points out that al-Ghazālī expresses this view only in the works which are meant for general consumption, whereas in other works he has disclosed the secret. Secondly, he shows al-Ghazālī's inconsistency in those very works where he employs *ta'wīl* in cetain matters which are not rationally impossible. Finally, he criticises the concept of *muḥāl* itself from two angles. At best it is a relative term, the referent of which may differ from person to person. Indeed, al-Ghazālī himself takes this factor into consideration and refrains from charging the Ḥanbalites with *kufr* for their belief that God is *dhū jihah* and *dhū ishārah*, because it is not rationally impossible, according to them.

"Surely this is very generous of the Imām Ṣāḥib [Shiblī says], but why should this generosity be limited to the Ḥanbalites? According to the philosophers of Islam, *i'ādah-i ma'dūm* is rationally impossible and, therefore, they do not believe in bodily resurrection. Why then does the Imām Ṣāḥib charge them with *kufr*?"

At worst the concept is inadequate, for it does not include the practically impossible and the improbable. Thus, except for a thing or two, everything is possible according to this concept. Such a thinking, Shiblī declares, is at the root of all kinds of superstitions among the Muslims today. Shiblī ends the discourse with this significant conclusion: "If a thing is mentioned in the *sharī'ah*, it is not necessary that it has an external existence."[108] In the following section he explains what kind of existence such non-material, non-sensible things may have.

A great many of "the apparently irrational things in the *sharī'ah*" Shiblī would explain as metaphorical expressions (such as the covenant of mankind with God in eternity, God's sitting on the throne, etc.) or as material expressions of spiritual things (such as reward and punishment

108. Ibid., pp. 171-97.

after death, etc.). But this still leaves out a great number of "those spiritual things or meanings (*rūḥāniyāt* or *ma'ānī*) which appear to the Prophets in material form". To explain these Shiblī makes use of what al-Ghazālī calls *wujūd-i ḥissī* or *tamaththul-i khayālī* (sensory existence or imaginative picturisation), what Shaykh al-Ishrāq calls *'ālam-i ashbāḥ* or *'ālam-i amthāl* (world of spirits or similitudes) and what Shāh Walī Allāh calls *'ālam-i mithāl* (world of images) and *ālam-i barzakh* (world of suspension?). Although these thinkers include in this category many eschatological matters, as well as *jinns* and devils (Shaykh al-Ishrāq), *mi'rāj*, etc. (Shāh Walī Allāh), Shiblī would include these things, if we have not misunderstood him, in the second category (i.e. material expressions of spiritual things) and would reserve the last category to explain the visions and auditions of the Prophets, that is, the reality of the angels and the revelation. It is not quite clear whether Shiblī is referring to the concepts of all three thinkers or only to that of al-Ghazālī when he explains the nature of the existence of the angels and of the phenomenon of revelation in these words: These things occur in a dream-like condition obtaining, due to deep concentration of the subject, in the state of being fully awake, in which the psyche or the imaginative power (*rūḥ yā nafs yā quwwat-i mutakhayyilah*) acts untrammelled by the ordinary senses. "No objection is brought against this *iḥtimāl,*" Shiblī says, "from the viewpoint of present-day sciences and philosophy." He concludes the section with this revealing remark: "Al Fārābī, Ibn Sīnā and others are of the same opinion, but we did not mention their elaborations because these people are not regarded as authoritative from a religious point of view."[109]

(8)

Although it was meant to be so, Shiblī's *Al-Kalām* was not destined to be the final statement of his views on the problems of a new, up-dated theology of Islam. It is perhaps not surprising that Shiblī's quest for a more satisfying *kalām* for his age should have eventually led him to Rūmī with whose ideas he had already become acquainted in the course of his earlier works on *kalām*. He had indeed argued from Rūmī's views on a few occasions.[110] He must have realised then the great potential of Rūmī or rather of his *Mathnawī* for the new *kalām*. But this was not perhaps the only reason why Shiblī ended up with Rūmī. He knew that a stage came in the history of the evolution of Islamic dogma when *falsafah* and *taṣawwuf* had merged into each other.[111] Consciously or unconsciously, he was probably himself heading in that direction. The mystical rationalism of Rūmī was thus only a logical next step from

109. Ibid., pp. 197-218.
110. Ibid., pp. 104, 209-12.
111. *'Ilm al-Kalām*, p. 16.

the philosophical rationalism of the Mu'tazilites and of the Muslim philosophers.

Although Shiblī did not—despite his initially stated view that science and religion are worlds apart from each other—miss the opportunity to point out in Rūmī's thought the germs of Darwinian evolutionism and certain other theories of modern science,[112] this was not what really attracted him to Rūmī. The magnetism of Rūmī lay in the fact that he, unlike the Ash'arites, succeeded in creating a feeling of credibility or plausibility (*idh'ān yā ẓann-i ghālib*) in the heart, which is "the limit of factuality in philosophical matters".[113] This Rūmī achieved by using *qiyās-i tamthīlī* instead of the usual *qiyās-i shumulī*.[114] Shiblī admits that it was not possible for Rūmī to be completely immune from the worldwide storm of Ash'arism and consequently he often based his doctrines on Ash'arite principles. "But," says Shiblī, "when he explains them, the upper layers continue to peel off and in the end only the core of the matter remains."[115]

Before going into those specific points of interest which Shiblī found in Rūmī's *Mathnawī*, one or two things should be clarified. Aziz Ahmad has claimed that

"Rūmī's *kalām*, as he [Shiblī] sums it up, . . . is based on an eclecticism which refuses to regard any religion as abso-

112. *Sawāniḥ*, pp. 219-24.
113. Ibid., p. 97 ; see also pp. 7, 121 f.
114. Ibid., pp. 98 ff.
115. Ibid., pp. 94 f.

lutely false, but considers that religions are mixed in various proportions with elements of falsehood and truth."[116]

This may be a true assessment of Rūmī's ***kalām***, but probably not of Shiblī's understanding of it, or at least of what he was trying to derive from it. Aziz Ahmad's statement seems all the more strange in view of the fact that the very first heading in the section of Shiblī's *Sawāniḥ Mawlānā Rūm* devoted to a topical study of Rūmī's ***kalām*** reads: "***madhāhib-i mukhtalifah men se ek na ek madhhab kā ṣaḥīḥ honā ḍarūr hay***". Below Shiblī argues from Rūmī against relativism in the matter of true and false religions.[117] His liberalism notwithstanding, we know that Shiblī never went to the extent of compromising the exclusiveness of Islam.

It is also not quite true to say that "it is to Rūmī that Shiblī turns in quest of an angelology and an eschatology more reconcilable with orthodoxy than those of Sayyid Aḥmad Khān."[118] Though Shiblī was not the one to shun additional support, particularly if it came from such a venerated person and Ash'arite as Rūmī, he had already dealt with these and various other questions of belief in his earlier works on ***kalām***.[119] What he discovered in Rūmī, if one were to believe Shiblī, was a better, more convincing way of argumenta-

116. Aziz Ahmad, op. cit., p. 85.

117. *Sawāniḥ*, pp. 123 f.

118. Aziz Ahmad, op. cit., p. 85.

119. See *'Ilm al-Kalām*, *Al-Ghazālī* and *Al-Kalām*, *passim*.

tion, a clearer, more appealing presentation of faith. For instance, on the question of resurrection (which, by the way, is the only part of eschatology dealt with in the context of Rūmī) Shiblī liked Rūmī's positive argument—which he presented over and above the usual negative argument from the imperishability of the soul. He liked the way Rūmī argued for the plausibility of resurrection from the process of evolution in life, a Darwinian as well as Qur'ānic concept, according to Shiblī. There is likely to be still another, better stage of life. This, Shiblī says, is in consonance with modern science which holds that matter and energy are indestructible. Body and soul will, thus, only assume another form.[120] Another instance of Shiblī's preference for Rūmīan interpretation is seen in the question of the reality of angels. Though Shiblī had already assigned them a dream-like existence, he goes further and clearly states with reference to Rūmī that they are nothing but powers emanating from man himself.[121] This can hardly be regarded as "more reconcilable with orthodoxy".

Perhaps the most important, substantive contribution that Rūmī made to Shiblī's theological thought was Rūmī's explanation of the cosmic order in which the concepts of soul and evolution played an important part. Rūmī viewed the cosmic order as denoting a progressive dematerialisation of

120. *Sawānih*, pp. 174-79. 121. Ibid., pp. 145-47.

things, called *tajarrud 'an al-māddah*. Beginning from the low, elemental stage of inanimate beings (*jamād*) and going through the first compound stage in plants (*nabāt*), things become less and less material as they go up and up; until they reach the animal (*ḥayawān*) stage where they acquire soul or perception. The evolution continues in the soul—the human soul and the prophetic soul being only stages in this process—till one arrives at the pure, sublime God.[122] Shiblī presents this scheme not so much as an argument for the existence of the Soul, Prophecy and God, as an effective means—if only one ponders the cosmic order—to combat the pervasiveness of materialism which is undermining the roots of religion. It has, however, been used by Rūmī, not without eliciting Shiblī's admiration, to prove the existence of God. The argument rests on learning through induction that less material things, which are also comparatively hidden, real and superior, are the cause of more material things in this world. The decreasing materiality of the causes continues in the upper reaches of the cosmic scale till one attains of necessity the absolutely non-material, non-sensible and most sublime existent, namely, God. Shiblī prefers this argument to those of the *mutakallimīn*, since it affirms not merely a cause of the causes but a God with sublime attributes.[123] Not less importantly, in Rūmī's concept of *waḥdat*

122. Ibid., pp. 162-72.

123. Ibid., pp. 126-30.

al-wujūd, Shiblī finally seems to find a satisfactory solution to the problem of how a world which is eternal can be still regarded as created by God. It can be so regarded because it is not an effect but a manifestation of an eternal God. "Thus, as far as *falsafah* is concerned," Shiblī says, "there is no alternative except for the doctrine of the Ṣūfīs." But even the *sharī'ah* and ***nuṣūṣ-i Qur'ānī*** are not against it.[124]

Generally noticeable in Shiblī's treatment of, and reliance upon, Rūmī is perhaps a more sober and mature stand on the specific problems of theology. The new trend is particularly evidenced by his treatment of the problem of predestination and free-will. Though he never regarded the controversy over this question a legitimate concern of ***kalām***, old or new, he was an earnest believer in the free-will of man, and harshly critical of the Ash'arites for their stand to the contrary. So is he even now. Underlining the necessity for holding man responsible for his actions, he goes on to cite from Rūmī one argument after another in support of his view. But now he at least realises the difficulties involved, on a psychological level, in exclusive assertion of or, for that matter, denial of free-will. Though predestination in an absolute sense is still out, since it goes against spontaneous intuition (***badāhah***), there is at least a case for it as a fact of human psychology.[125]

124. Ibid., pp. 204-06.

125. Ibid., pp. 185-94.

Finally, there is also noticeable on a still more general level a subtle but unmistakable shift of emphasis in Shiblī's overall attitude towards the problem of reason and faith, or science and religion. Shiblī had never asked for scientific certainty in the matter of religious beliefs. He, in fact, started with an attempt to differentiate between the quality of scientific and religious truths. By the time he reached Rūmī he seems to have become more convinced of the fact that one can never establish religious truths in any scientific sense; one can only create necessary conditions for beliefs. What really matters is that man should be persuaded to believe by showing the plausibility of religious truths, by appealing to his common sense and feeling. In short, religious truths are not empirical but emotive. Perhaps most important in connection with this is Shiblī's realisation that, in the final analysis, the hold of naturalism and materialism over the minds of men must be weakened—perhaps through mystical-philosophical contemplation—if religion as a transcendental concept is to stay, and if the idea of a living and personal God is to play any role in the life of man.[126]

126. Ibid., pp. 130 f.

II

Changing Law

(1)

If one were to characterise Shiblī's thinking on Islamic law rather superficially, one could sum it up just by saying that Shiblī was a Ḥanafite.[1] He started as a conscious Ḥanafite and died as such. His earliest known writings, *Ẓill al Ghamām fī Mas'alat al-Qir'at Khalf al Imām* (in Urdu) and (*Iskāt al-Mu'tadī 'alā Inṣāt al-Muqtadī* (in Arabic), were written in support of Ḥanafism and in refutation of *Ahl-i Ḥadīth* or *ghayr muqallidīn*.[2] A few months before his death he declared in a statement about his beliefs that "I am a Ḥanafite both in beliefs and in juristic matters".[3] But a closer look reveals that except for the name almost nothing was common between his earlier and later Ḥanafism. He may have remained a *ghālī* Ḥanafite to the last,[4] but the meaning and content of his

1. The *nisbah* Nu'mānī is a token of Shiblī's devotion to Ḥanafism and its founder. Sayyid Sulaymān Nadwī, *Ḥayāt*, p. 69.
2. Ibid., pp. 100-07.
3. Ibid., pp. 822 f.
4. Ibid., p. 816.

Ḥanafism had undergone a radical change with the passage of time. The beginning was so rigid and conservative that, according to him, a person could become a Christian but not a *ghayr muqallid.*[5] The end was so flexible and liberal that perhaps the single most important reason why he still liked to call himself a Ḥanafite was that, according to him, Ḥanafism eminently symbolised consideration for this-worldly human needs and was best suited for culturally more advanced societies; in other words, because it stood for change and progress.[6]

In the earlier works of Shiblī mentioned above his Ḥanafism manifested itself in the confutation of the *ghayr muqallidīn* and that too in a very trivial matter. But about ten years after, his Ḥanafism appears in *Sīrat al-Nu'mān* in a positive manner.[7] In this work Shiblī employs his forceful pen not in disputation with *Ahl-i Ḥadīth*, but in arguing that Ḥanafite law, which for him is Islamic law *par excellence* in that it was Abū Ḥanīfah who laid the foundations of the science of *fiqh* in Islam,[8] is not essentially derived from Roman law, and that it rather had in itself the

5. Muḥammad Mahdī, *Tadhkirah-i Shams al-'Ulamā'*, p. 6; also quoted in Shaykh Muḥammad Ikrām, *Shiblī Nāmah*, p. 33.

6. *Al-Nu'mān*, p. 267.

7. In his review on this book, Ḥālī praises it as a pioneering work which "lays the foundation of the philosophy of religion in our [Urdu] literature". *Maqālāt-i Ḥālī*, II, 166.

8. *Al-Nu'mān*, pp. 246, 251 ff., 275 ff.

necessary materials and conditions for genesis and growth[9]—a clear advance, in fact a jump, in Shiblī's outlook, concern and thinking. Whether the worshipper should or should not recite the first *sūrah* of the Qur'ān behind the leader of the congregational prayer, is no more the bone of contention with *Ahl-i Ḥadīth.*[10] What Shiblī is out to show now is that the Ḥanafite law is pre-eminently characterised by reason, facility, expansion and, especially, progress with civilisation.[11] Perhaps in Abū Ḥanīfah he is subconsciously looking for a support for the destined reformulation of the Islamic law in accordance with the needs of the modern age; just as he found in al-Ghazālī a prop for the reconstruction of Islamic theology.[12]

(2)

Although Shiblī shows the reasonableness and facility of Ḥanafite law in matters of ritual,[13] he

9. Ibid., pp. 283-95, *et passim.*

10. He mentions it only casually in the course of his narration of the instances of Abū Ḥanīfah's use of reason, as he also mentions the questions of *raf'-i yadayn* and *āmīn bi al-jahr*. *Al-Nu'mān*, pp. 110-13, 337 f., 343. Also see *Al-Kalām*, pp. 221 f.

11. *Al-Nu'mān*, pp. 296-330.

12. Indeed, Shiblī here relates Abū Ḥanīfah's rationalism to the fact that he started his codification of *fiqh* with a background in *'ilm al-kalām* and discussions with the Mu'tazilites, as compared to other *faqīhs* who started with the problems of *fiqh* themselves. He even ascribes the irrationalism of Ash'arite *kalām* to the fact that Abū al-Ḥasan al-Ash'arī was a follower of al-Shāfi'ī who was inclined towards irrationalism in matters of *fiqh*. *Al-Nu'mān*, pp. 296 f., 299; also pp. 40 f, 151 f.

13. Ibid., pp. 296-304.

is more concerned with that aspect of it which deals with social relations, crimes and punishments, and judicial procedures—in this order. "A very great part of *fiqh* with which the worldly needs are related is that of *mu'āmalāt*," he writes, "and it is here that the subtleness and ingenuity of a *mujtahid* can be fully judged."[14] It goes without saying that Abū Ḥanīfah would come out the winner in comparison with others. Shiblī selects a few test-cases to show that the Ḥanafite law is pre-eminently in consonance with civilisation and refinement.

It need hardly be pointed out that the selection of the cases as well as the criteria on which he judged them are both influenced, if not exactly determined, by the priorities and values of Western liberalism. Shiblī takes up the institution of marriage and shows that "even in the most civilised countries of today the rules of marriage are no better than those in Ḥanafite *fiqh*". Indeed as compared to the Roman law whose rules of marriage are, according to Bentham, a "collection of injustices," the Ḥanafite rules of marriage are a "collection of justices". The main point he emphasises is that in all the rules of marriage Abū Ḥanīfah has taken into consideration the principle of the equality of man and woman "which distinguishes his *fiqh* from that of the other *a'immah* in this matter". Indeed, according to

14. Ibid., p. 308.

Abū Ḥanīfah, a single woman's witness in matters of marriage, divorce, etc., is as reliable as that of a single man; and a woman can even be appointed to the post of *qāḍī*. A woman who has reached the age of maturity has the same right as a man to contract her own marriage, and to dissolve it if contracted by the guardian in her immaturity. A woman has the right to *khula'* without paying any compensation if the man is in the wrong. When it comes to the laws of divorce which are rather strict in Ḥanafite *fiqh*, Shiblī manages to find yet another civilisational principle behind them, namely, that marriage should be a strong and durable contract.[15]

Another evidence of the civility of the Ḥanafite law, in fact one of its chief characteristics, is the generous rights it has given to non-Muslims living in a Muslim state, which "no government in the world has ever given to an alien people; Europe, which is proud of its law and justice, can make verbal claims, but cannot offer actual examples". Again, the main thing emphasised is the general legal equality of Muslims and non-Muslims, particularly in the matter of punishment for murder. In his generosity Abū Ḥanīfah indeed crossed the limit of moderation when he ruled that the contract of protection will not be regarded as void until and unless non-Muslims ganged up against the government. At

15. Ibid., pp. 310-21; also see pp. 353-56.

this point Shiblī recalls those harsh and illiberal regulations against non-Muslims which are found in Ḥanafite works such as *Hidāyah* (and *Fatāwā-i 'Ālamgīrī* which contains still more severe regulations) and which are reportedly purported to achieve the humiliation of non-Muslims. At first Shiblī tries to save the situation by saying that these illiberal regulations are the invention of the jurists of later times (***muta'akhkhirīn***), and thus Abū Ḥanīfah could not be blamed for them. But Shiblī cannot ignore the fact that part of them is reported from Abū Ḥanīfah himself, and with some additions also from Abū Yūsuf who attributes them to 'Umar I. Shiblī accepts this and turns the discussion around the question whether 'Umar issued these regulations to humiliate non-Muslims or to keep them apart from Muslims. In Shiblī's view it was for the latter reason that 'Umar issued these regulations. The reason, furthermore, was a matter of 'Umar's personal taste and hence, Shiblī means, lacking permanent legal value.[16]

Still another proof of the civility and mildness of the Ḥanafite law is its rules pertaining to punishments. For instances, Abū Ḥanīfah adds so many qualifications to the definition of theft that the punishment by amputation of the hand of the thief cannot be carried out easily. According to Abū Ḥanīfah, punishment for murder is the same

16. Ibid., pp. 322-30.

for everyone, whether he or she is free or slave, Muslim or non-Muslim; and wilful murder must be punished by execution and not by blood-money.[17]

Shiblī is very keen to show the modernity of the Ḥanafite as compared to other schools of law; but one should note that he is no less concerned with showing that it is also more close to the tradition—to the correct meaning of the Qur'ān and also, contrary to the general belief, to the true *ḥadīth* This, as a matter of fact, he regards as one of the chief characteristics of the Ḥanafite law, and discusses it in sufficient detail.[18]

(3)

Although Shiblī has underlined the true-to-modernity-and-tradition character of the actual content of the Ḥanafite law, the point he is perhaps more concerned with is that due to the peculiarly urban and civilised circumstances in which it originally evolved at the hands of Abū Ḥanīfah—whose own ingenuity played no small role in its development—the Ḥanafite law came to acquire certain characteristics or principles which were conducive to further legislation suitable to the ever-new needs and demands of a developing society.[19] The basic and most telling of these principles of law-making as evolved by Abū Ḥanīfah is, according to Shiblī, the distinction

17. Ibid., pp. 305-07, 347-51.
18. Ibid., pp. 330-57.
19. See above, refs. 8 and 9.

which Abū Ḥanīfah made between legislative and non-legislative commands, particularly in respect of the *Ḥadīth*.[20] But others, as we shall see, turn out to be hardly less important.

Shiblī must have been well aware of the crucial importance of clearly defining the role of *Ḥadīth* in the process of law-making. He devotes seventy-five pages of *Sīrat al-Nu'mān*[21] ostensibly to show that Abū Ḥanīfah, contrary to the prevalent notion, did not disregard *Ḥadīth* as a source of law.[22] But with undisguised appreciation Shiblī shows in great detail how cautious and critical Abū Ḥanīfah was in accepting a *ḥadīth* as true and binding—something which led to a radical curtailment of the use of *Ḥadīth* material.[23]

Tracing the gradual evolution of *Ḥadīth* material and narration from its very small beginning under the Prophet and underlining the discouragement of its use especially by 'Umar I, on the one hand, and demonstrating the increasing numbers of *aḥādīth* due to fabrications and careless narrations after the *fitnah*, on the other, Shiblī contends that

> "the volume of *Ḥadīth* material which had already come into existence by the time of Abū Ḥanīfah was full of fabricated, erroneous, weak and interpolated Traditions . . . he laid the foundation of the criticism of Traditions and established its principles, and rules."[24]

20. *Al-Nu'mān*, p. 269.
21. Ibid., pp. 170-245.
22. Ibid., pp. 170-85.
23. Ibid., pp. 186-245.
24. Ibid., pp. 186-95.

For instance, Abū Ḥanīfah held that "only that *ḥadīth* is authoritative which the narrator heard himself and remembered till the time of narration," even if he had it in writing[25] Though he accepted ***riwāyat bi al-ma'nī***, he limited it to the Companions and the Successors and tended to further condition it with *tafaqquh*.[26] Moreover, Abū Ḥanīfah also applied the principles of ***dirāyat*** in *Ḥadīth* criticism. For instance, he held that "a ***ḥadīth*** which is against irrefutable reason (*'aql-i qaṭ'ī*) is not trustworthy"; or, that "a Tradition which is not higher than ***akhbār-i aḥād*** in status will be doubtful if it relates such events as occur daily to all the people."[27] Finally, he used the hidden reason (***'illat-i khafiyyah***)—for which a knack or taste is developed through constantly looking into the underlying reasons and ultimate causes (*asrār-o maṣāliḥ*) of the *sharī'ah*—in judging the veracity of Traditions.[28]

The application of these principles cut down quite drastically the amount of ***Ḥadīth*** material accepted as useful and reliable.[29] But Abū Ḥanīfah did not stop here.

"There is not the slightest difference [Shibli says] between the *Ḥadīth* and the Qur'ān from the point of view of their authoritative nature; one is recited revelation (*waḥy matlū'*) and the other is unrecited (*ghayr matlū'*). Whatever difference

25. Ibid., pp. 199 ff., 203.
26. Ibid., pp. 209 f., 203-08.
27. Ibid., pp. 214 ff., 216 ff.
28. Ibid., pp. 221-26.
29. Ibid., pp. 200-03, 209 f., 214-16, 224, 226.

there may be is seen in the proof of the authenticity of a *ḥadīth*; if a *ḥadīth* is attested with the same incess ncy and certainty as the Qur'ān, then it is equal to the Qur'ān in the establishment of the commands. But the degrees of the authenticity of the *Ḥadīth* are different; and these differences need to be taken into account in the establishment of the commands."

Abū Ḥnīfah, accordingly, graded the *aḥādīth*, with respect to their authenticity and their legal effectiveness, into *mutawātir*, *mashhūr* and *aḥād*. While *mutawātir* can establish *farḍīyyah* and *ruknīyyah*, and *mashhūr* can restrict an unrestricted command in the Qur'ān and make an addition to it, *aḥād*, since it is *ẓannī al thubūt*, can have no effect on the textual (*manṣūṣah*) commands of the Qur'ān.[30] This, in effect, meant that a legist could have more discretion in arriving at legal judgments, since *Ḥadīth* material comprises overwhelmingly these *akhbār-i aḥād*.

Shiblī devotes full fifteen pages to discussing and demonstrating on his own the assumptions involved at various levels in the affirmation of *akhbār-i aḥād*. Thus he demolishes the connectedness (*ittiṣāl*) of the *marfū'* and *ma'an'an* Traditions on this basis, and also shows the assumptive nature of the *rijāl* criticism on which rest all the *akhbār-i aḥād*. Finally, *riwāyat bi al-ma'nā*, which accounts for the majority of such *aḥādīth*, is in itself pregnant with all kinds of assumptions.

30. Ibid., pp. 226 ff.

"The attitude which Abū Ḥanīfah adopted in this matter was [according to Shiblī] very moderate, and a proof of the finesse of his mind; he neither rejected them totally, like the Mu'tazilites, nor accepted them as certain with the credulity of the superficial observers."[31]

On this already severely reduced material of true and binding *aḥādith* Shiblī brings into play Abū Ḥanīfah's distinction between legislative (*tashrī'ī*) and non legislative (*ghayr tashrī'ī*) commands and *aḥādīth*, which further cuts into the authenticated but graded *Ḥadīth* material. He introduces the subject with a reference to Shāh Walī Allāh who also made a similar distinction among the *aḥādīth*, setting off those which are the proper concern of Prophethood (indicated by the Qur'ānic verse: *mā ātākumu al Rasūl fa khudhūhu wa mā nahākum 'anhu fa intahū*) from those which are not (indicated by the Prophetic Tradition: *innamā anā basharun idhā amartukum bi shay'in min dīnikum fakhudhūhuwaidhāamartukum bi shay'in min ra'yī fa innamā anā bashar*). In the second category he included things such as what the Prophet did habitually (*'ādatan*) or accidentally (*ittifāqan*) or said in accordance with the ideas of his people; or adopted on account of partial exigency (*maṣlaḥat-i juz'ī*), which is not binding on all the people; for example, the prescription of a rite (*shi'ār kī ta'yīn*). It is because of the latter that 'Umar I said: "Why should we

31. Ibid., pp. 231-45.

do *ramal* now, when God destroyed the people for whose benefit we used to do it?" Many other commands of the Prophet fall into this category; for instance, his command that "the person who slays an infidel in battle will be the owner of his arms."[32]

Shāh Walī Allāh was an example nearer home, but the credit for first conceiving of distinction between legislative and non-legislative *aḥādīth* goes, according to Shiblī, to Abū Ḥanīfah. It was on account of this distinction that Abū Ḥanīfah regarded the *aḥādīth* concerning the major ritual ablution on Friday, the women's going out to 'Īd prayers, the effectuation of divorce, the fixing of poll tax, the designation of the tribute and the distribution of the booty as non-legislative. "The great advantage which the Ḥanafite law has over against laws of other schools is," according to Shiblī, "that its rules are generally based on this priniciple. That is the reason why it has that expansiveness and freedom which are lacking in the rules of other *a'immah.*" Abū Ḥanīfah adopted this principle, Shiblī believes, because he had the precedents of the Pious Caliphs before him, by which Shiblī mostly means what are generally known as *awwalīyāt-i 'Umar I*. These include: 'Umar's interdiction against the sale and purchase of *ummahāt-i awlād*; 'Umar's conversion of "three divorces" into definite divorce; and Abū Bakr's setting forty lashes as punishment for

32. Ibid., pp. 269-71.

drinking and then 'Umar's raising it to eighty. In such matters the Pious Caliphs acted against the Prophet's commands knowing that they were not legislative.[33]

At this point the question may arise: how one did or could distinguish between legislative and non-legislative *aḥādīth*? Shiblī had probably this question in mind when he wrote that because of their constant association with the Prophet, the Companions "had become cognizant of the nuances of the *sharī'ah* and it was very easy for them to distinguish the legislative commands from those that fell in the category regarding which the Prophet had said: ***antum a'lamu bi umūri dunyākum***. That is how (namely, by following the method of the Companions) Abū Ḥanīfah distiguished between the two,[34] and that is perhaps how Shiblī would want us to distinguish between the two. We shall have more to say on this later. At the moment we should part company with Abū Ḥanīfah and go along with Shiblī to Shāh Walī Allāh, whose importance we have already seen in connection with the distinction between legislative and non-legislative *aḥadīth*, for a still more revolutionary principle of law-making in Islam.

(4)

Having dealt with the *Ḥadīth* material in the

33. Ibid., pp. 271-73.
34. Ibid., pp. 273 f.; also see p. 272.

manner described above, Shiblī was still left with a great deal of material, Traditional as well as Qur'ānic, which looked indisputably legislative in nature, and which posed difficult problems in this civilised, progressive world of his. In order to find a way, to put it rather bluntly, around the implications of this material, he fell back upon the role of usages and customs in the formation of the *sharī'ah*. We have already seen in the previous chapter[35] how Shiblī referred to Shāh Walī Allāh in his argument for keeping the respective domains of religion and science apart. There, only the things which did not pertain to the refinement of the self (*tahdhīb al-nafs*) and administration of the community (*siyāsat al-ummah*)—such as natural, and even historical, events—were not the proper concern of the Prophets. Now it was the turn of the *sharī'ah* itself, and the question was how much of it was religiously relevant and binding.

In a section of his *Al-Kalām* entitled "Prophets' method of instruction and guidance,"[36] Shiblī develops his ideas on the universals and particulars in the *sharī'ahs* of the Prophets in general and the *sharī'ah* of the Prophet Muḥammad in particular, with the help of Shāh Walī Allāh. Quoting extensively from Shāh Walī Allāh's *Ḥujjat Allāh al-Bālighah* at every stage, Shiblī first establishes the principle that in the formulation of their respective *sharī'ahs*, the Prophets adopt and preach,

35. See above, pp. 6-7.

36. *Al-Kalām*, pp. 108-15.

with suitable (but never radical, and only when necessary) changes, the social, economic, judicial and other usages and customs of the people to whom they are sent.[37] Then Shiblī goes on to distinguish between two parts of the *sharī'ahs*. One, those beliefs and matters which constitute the universal principles of religion and in respect of which the *sharī'ahs* are united, such as the existence and unity of God, reward and punishment in the Hereafter, worship, veneration for *sha'ā'ir Allāh*, marriage, inheritance, etc. Two, those rules and practices which are particular to various Prophets and on the basis of which it is said, for instance, that the *sharī'ah* of Moses is different from that of Jesus. This part of *sharī'ahs* is based on the requirements and interests of specific peoples or countries, and is founded mainly on those ideas, beliefs, habits, business relations, conventions, way of living and principle of civilisation which already exist in that people.

"That was the reason [Shiblī quotes directly from Shāh Walī Allāh] why camels' meat was prescribed to Banī Isrā'īl but not to Banī Ismā'īl; why the distinction between good and bad food was made in consideration of the habits of the Arabs; and why marriage with the sister's daughter was forbidden in our religion but not among the Jews."[38]

As long as the Prophets were being sent to specific peoples, they could formulate their *sharī'ahs* with special consideration to the customs and

37. Ibid., pp. 108 f.

38. Ibid., pp. 109-11.

characteristics of those peoples; and that was that. But this principle cannot work in the method of instruction of a Prophet who is sent to the whole world, Shiblī argues following Shāh Walī Allāh, since he can neither formulate separate *sharī'ahs* for all the different peoples of the world, nor can the customs and characteristics of all these peoples conform with each other. Consequently, he starts with the instruction and education of his own people and makes them a model of good morals; this people serve as his limbs, and on its pattern he goes on widening the circle of his instruction. Although his *sharī'ah* mostly contains those universal rules and general principles which are common to almost all the peoples of the world, yet the consideration of the customs and characteristics of his own people is prominent. But the ordinances which are formed on the basis of these customs and conditions are neither meant to be an end in themselves (*maqṣūd bi al-dhāt*) nor are they much emphasised. To quote Shāh Walī Allāh's own words:

"Therefore, there is not a better and simpler way than to take into consideration, in matters of *sha'ā'ir*, *ḥudūd* and *irtifāqāt*, the customs of the people to whom he [a Prophet? The Prophet?] is sent; and the people coming after should not be pressed hard about these matters."[39]

This led Shiblī to conclude finally that

39. Ibid., pp. 113 f.

"it will become apparent from this principle, to what extent the customs of Arabia have been taken into consideration in determining the punishments in Islamic *sharī'ah* of theft, fornication, murder, etc., and how far it is necessary to be bound with exactly the same, specific punishments."[40]

These words speak for themselves and hardly need any comment. However, one should mention as a matter of record that, though Shiblī never spelled out positively his attitude towards the Qur'ān as a source of law, he obviously did not regard the Qur'ānic ***nuṣūṣ***, at least those which pertained to criminal law, as final and eternal.

(5)

Shiblī had come a long way from petty squabbling in defence of the Ḥanafite position on minor points of law to raising fundamental questions of lasting value about the principles of law-making in Islam. This should not, however, give the impression that he had cut himself off from Ḥanafism. In the first place, he had no reason to do so inasmuch as he believed that the Ḥanafite law, if any, was the most suitable one for the changing times. Secondly, we know that in his last article on law, "Masā'il-i Fiqhīyyah par Zamāne kī Ḍarūraton

40. Ibid., p. 115. See also Aziz Ahmad, *Islamic Modernism,* p. 255 Cf. Mi'rāj Muḥammad, "Shāh Walī Allāh's Attempt to Reconcile the Schools of Fiqh," Unpublished M.A. Thesis, McGill University, Montreal, 1968, pp. 49-55, for an interpretation of Shāh Walī Allāh on this point, contradicting the one made by Shiblī and other modernists, such as Iqbal.

kā Athar,"[41] Shiblī again fell back upon a Ḥanafite jurist, and a very late one at that, namely, Ibn al-'Ābidīn Shāmī (1784-1836), to seek support for his stand on the role of changing customs and needs in law-making. Two things should, however, be noted here. One, that not once does Shiblī refer to the fact that Shāmī is a Ḥanafite, or even give the slightest impression of promoting the cause of Ḥanafism. Two, that the thing uppermost in his mind is the Islamic law as such in relation to the changing times.

Shiblī begins the article thus:

> "Our opponents have said it hundreds of times before and say it even now that *Islām kā qanūn* (*masā'il-i fiqhīyyah*) is a dead limb (*dast-i shall*) which cannot move by any means; that is, it does not have the capacity for progress and, therefore, cannot go along with the needs of the time."[42]

Responding to the objection that his counterstand in this matter is "the result of the new ideas, otherwise, according to the ancients of Islam, there is no room for modification and alteration in the matter of *fiqh*," Shiblī comes up with Shāmī to vindicate his position. The article consists mostly of quotes from two treatises by Shāmī, especially his *Nashr al-'Urf fī Binā' Ba'ḍ al-Aḥkām 'alā al-'Urf*.[43]

The effect to which Shiblī is quoting Shāmī is that, except for those which are established by

41. *Maqālāt*, I, 75-81. 42. Ibid., I, 75. 43. Ibid.

a clear ***naṣṣ***, the rest of the ***masā'il i fiqhīyyah***, which are established by ***ijtihād*** and ***rā'y*** and are mostly based on the custom of the ***mujtahid's*** time, will change with the change of time,

"either because of the alteration of custom or the occurrence of a new need or the corruption of the people. For [the quotation continues] if the earlier ruling persisted, it would result in hardship and harm to the people, and in opposition to the fundamentals of the *sharī'ah*, which are based on relief and facilitation and removal of harm and corruption."[44]

After giving a few examples from Shāmī of change of rules on account of the change of customs,[45] Shiblī raises the question, again following Shāmī: "If the rulings of the ***sharī'ah*** can change with the change of time, where will this process end? Can it not encroach upon the religious duties themselves? Can the duties and pillars (*farā'iḍ awr arkān*) also change with the change of time?" The answer is: If the new custom is not incompatible with ***al-dalīl al-shar'ī*** in so absolute a manner as to necessitate the abandonment of the ***naṣṣ*** (for instance, in cases where ***dalīl*** is general or analogical), then the custom will be upheld, provided it is common, as the particulariser (***mukhaṣṣiṣ***) of ***al-dalīl al-shar'ī***.[46]

At this point we should ask a question ourselves: why has Shiblī gone to all this trouble of quoting extensively from Shāmī? Not, we believe,

44. Ibid., I, 75 f. 45. Ibid., I, 77. 46. Ibid., I, 78-80.

because he was interested in establishing the finality and permanent validity of the *nuṣūṣ*. But because he wanted to stress the principle of movement and change in the Islamic law, and to avail of still another device for making new adjustments with progressing time. He says in conclusion:

"After these clear statements who can claim that Islamic law lacks the capacity to progress and to conform with the needs of the time. Hundreds and thousands of particular matters relating to *mu'āmalāt*, which have come into existence these days, are declared lawful or unlawful simply because they are subordinated to some old general principles; otherwise, it is obvious that these particular matters did not exist at that time. But 'Allāmah Shāmī has proved on the basis of hundreds of Traditions that the application of the general principles (*kullīyāt*) is restricted due to common custom."[47]

Thus by limiting the role of *Ḥadīth* and enlarging the role of custom (*'ādah, 'urf*) in the process of law-making, Shiblī has, perhaps unwittingly, thrown the field of fresh legislation in Islam wide open. From his point of view there seems hardly any part of *sharī'ah*, at least in the socio-economic domain, which is not subject to change. This is not surprising in view of the fact that to him Islam essentially meant beliefs, rituals, and morals.[48]

47. Ibid., I, 80 f.

48. *Al-Kalām*, p. 1. He writes at another place: "The task of religion is to purify the soul and cure the spiritual maladies. But just as a straw, in order to grow and develop, needs the whole magnificent structure of the world, so the religion also has to do with politics, civilisation, philosophy, in short, every branch of life; and the root

Under the aggressive attacks of the Western critics of Islam, he was virtually forced to take up arms and to show the excellence of the age-old social institutions of Islam by contemporary Western standrads and value criteria. Put on the defensive he even went to the extent of deliberately making the socio-legal institutions of Islam an essential part of his new *kalām*.[49] Left alone, he, and perhaps many others, would have responded differently, more creatively to the intellectual-cultural stimuli of the West.[50]

But the question still remains: how far would Shiblī have gone? Was there anything of lasting, universal value in the societal norms of Islamic *sharī'ah*? Put like that, Shiblī would surely have answered the question in the affirmative. What he would not have found easy to specify, perhaps no one who has once been exposed to the human flux called history could, is the name of that something universal and lasting. Any decision in this regard would remain, in the final analysis, arbit-

and basis of all these exists in the teachings of the principles of Islam" (*Khuṭbāt*, p. 161). It would take a Mawdūdī to turn this organic relationship between spiritual and material to an almost mechanical one.

49. See above, p. 46. Also see *Al-Kalām*, pp. 143-67. In fact, at one point he refers to them as the subject-matter of an entirely new theology (*bilkul nayā 'ilm-i kalām*) of Islam (ibid., p. 6).

50. Cf. Fazlur Rahman, *Islam*, p. 213; *idem*, "Revival and Reform in Islam," op. cit., II, 641; W.C. Smith, *Islam in Modern History*, p. 92; *idem*, "Islam Confronted by Western Secularism: Revolutionary Reaction," in Dorothea Seelye Franck, Ed., *Islam in the Modern World*, p. 25.

rary in the sense that it would primarily be based on practical considerations of an ever-changing world.

(6)

We saw above how Shiblī effectively curtailed the all-inclusiveness of Islamic law and "floated" the normative in it; so much so that in the end its formulation was, in effect, left to the whims of a changing time or, to put it more appropriately, made consequent upon the dialogue between human reason and God's will. This was the position Shiblī had taken in principle or would seem to have taken by the logic of his own statements. Let us now see how he stands in relation to the actual social-legal problems of his day, particularly in relation to the sensitive question of women's liberation. Does he abide by the fluid principle that "the expediencies (*maṣlaḥaten*) of the *sharī'ah* are bound up with time and the time is bound up with them"?[51] To anticipate the conclusion, let us state that on the whole he does.

We have already seen Shiblī vaguely trying to show the equality of man and woman in the Ḥanafite law.[52] That was insignificant in comparison with his more substantive ideas on the question of women's education and social participation. While his views on the former are too

51. *Bāqīyāt*, p. 22.

52. See above, pp. 60-61.

unequivocally stated to leave any doubt in the matter, his stand on the latter has been thrown into confusion on account of an article entitled "*Pardah awr Islām*" which Shiblī wrote in the latter period of his life.[53] On the basis of this article and a few other statements of his it is generally believed and claimed that Shiblī was not only a staunch supporter of *pardah*, but also regarded it as a precept of Islam in the implied sense that it was of a permanent legal value.[54] Nothing can be farther from the true intent of Shiblī here or elsewhere. On a superficial reading of the said article one may tend to regard it as an inconsistent, conservative piece in an otherwise fairly modern, liberal composition of Shiblī's thought. One may even be tempted to explain it away simply by saying that since at the time when he wrote it Shiblī was trying to work in and through the '*ulamā*', therefore, he made an expedient concession to them. We need not resort to such devices since a close perusal of the article reveals that he did not actually compromise his position.

It should be noted that the article was written as a belated answer to an article by Ameer Ali published in one of the issues of the journal *Nineteenth Century* of the year 1899. In his article Ameer Ali had stated that the institution of *pardah* was a very late development in Islam, beginning, in

53. *Maqālāt*, I, 103-20.

54. Sayyid Sulaymān Nadwī, as quoted in Shaykh Muḥammad Ikrām, op. cit., p. 157.

fact, in the middle of the seventh century of *Hijrah*, with the coming of the Mongol "strangers" and the distintegration of the Caliphate. Ameer Ali further maintained that in the days of the Caliphs the women of the higher class used to appear before men without the cloak (*burqa'*).[55] Shiblī is taking issue with Ameer Ali on these two points. He demonstrates at length, on the one hand, that *pardah* in its various forms—and not always exclusively for women either—existed in Arabia long before Islam and was regularised and made compulsory by it, and, on the other hand, that it was precisely among the upper-class women that it was particularly in vogue as compared to the lower-class women and slave-girls.[56] Thus Shiblī is interested here, and he says as much, in the "historical aspect" of the problem and in rectifying a misconception as to the abiding practice in the entire Muslim world concerning *pardah*.[57] Indeed, he makes it clear at the very outset that "if the matter had been discussed from a rational standpoint, then we would not have felt the need to intervene; but it is also claimed that Islam does not prescribe it and, more than that, it was not conventionalised in the early centuries of Islam".[58] It can be noticed that Shiblī is simply stating that *pardah* is a religious injunction, and that, too, more as a fact of history than as a fact

55. *Maqālāt*, I, 103.
56. Ibid., I, 105-12, 115.
57. Ibid., I, 104.
58. Ibid., I, 103.

of religion. At any rate, nowhere does he say that it is absolute or unchangeable. In fact, if one may be permitted to draw any conclusion from the fact that Shiblī is linking the origin and development of the idea and institution of *pardah* with the evolving social distinctions and protectivism, following in the wake of the onward march of civilisation, we would say that he was not inclined towards bestowing a permanent character upon *pardah*.[59] This should take care, for the time being, of the legal aspect of the issue. Not less instructive is it to find out Shiblī's personal leanings in this matter.

Although Shiblī has avoided making any moral judgment in favour of or against *pardah* in this article, he has not been so reticent elsewhere. In his *Safarnāmah* Shiblī wrote very favourably of the loose silken gown, head-cover and the fine muslin kerchief over the lower half of the face, which the Turkish women put on when going out. He, indeed, refers to two young Turkish girls, who were introduced to him, as "goddesses of chastity".[60] On the other hand, he also applauds the Begam of Bhopal for managing the affairs of the state from behind the *pardah*. "The example of the esteemed lady is a rejoinder to those who assert that women cannot become proficient remaining in *pardah*," he says.[61] Likewise, Shiblī commends in the same breath Qāsim Amīn's *Taḥrīr*

59. Ibid., I, 103-08.
60. *Safarnāmah*, pp. 131 f.
61. *Maqālāt*, VIII, 109.

al-Mar'ah and *al-Mar'at al-Jadīdah* as well as Faiīd Wajdī's *Al-Mar'at al-Muslimah* which was written as a rebuttal to Qāsim Amīn.[62] One may well ask what Shiblī is trying to prove by making now one statement, now another. The answer probably is that the poor man was caught in the middle. While this may partly be due to a genuine intellectual dilemma as to what is more useful for the society, it must partly also be due to the sensitiveness and the immediate social relevance of the issue of ***pardah*** in the conservative Indian Muslim society in general, and in the circles of ***'ulamā'***, among whom during the last years of his life Shiblī was trying to achieve a breakthrough,[63] in particular. When one deals with *'ulamā'*, one is virtually walking on eggs. Shiblī had to adopt a cautious line. He must have been half out of his wits trying to keep the precarious balance between his personal inclinations and an unreceptive audience. That is probably what gave birth to such

62. *Makātīb*, I, 234; *Maqālāt*, V, 136-38.

63. In a letter to his friend, Mahdī Ḥasan, Shiblī discloses that his plan to revolutionise the thinking of *'ulamā'* can be accomplished only in stages "... If I had shown my hand in *Ghazālī*, *'ulamā'* would have been lost to me for years, even for generations to come; and I do not want to cut myself off from them" (Shaykh Muḥammad Ikrām, op. cit., p. 113). Shiblī advised Abū al-Kalām to maintain the guise of *mawlawīyyat*, as it may be usefully employed (ibid., pp. 176 f.). Interesting though the idea may be, it will be an exaggeration to hold, as S.A.A. Rizvi does, that "Shiblī ... had come to believe that an oligarchy of the *'ulamā'* under his own leadership might control the Indian Muslim politics" ("The Breakdown of Traditional Society," *Cambridge History of Islam*, II, 93).

disparate statements. What is remarkable, however, is that he was still able to commend Qāsim Amīn's works which were generally condemned in Egypt itself until as late as 1918.[64] As a matter of fact, Shiblī was able to do much more than that. People may have different views about Shiblī's stand regarding *pardah*, but there cannot be two opinions about his very modern and liberal ideas on the education and social participation of women—omelets he could probably make without breaking the eggs.

In the above-mentioned article Shiblī makes a distinction between applications of the word *pardah*: one in the sense of the covering of the face and body, which was a pre-Islamic custom; and the other in the sense of segregation from the male sex, which did not exist in pre-Islamic Arabia. While he mentions that *pardah* in the former sense was adopted in Islam, Shiblī leaves out, purposely we think, any discussion of the *pardah* in Islam in the latter sense.[65] This should be taken to mean that Shiblī was making an exception of it. This inference has at least as much validity as the other inference that he was in favour of covering the face and body. But we have more positive and direct evidence on the subject. In the "civilisation and progress" of the contemporary Turks the one thing which Shiblī finds "most valuable and

64. *Musalmān 'Awrat kī Āzādī*, p. 7 of the Introduction.
65. *Maqālāt*, I, 105-08.

worthy of imitation" is the "women's education and social conduct". Why? Because, in Shiblī's opinion, it follows a middle course between the objectionable extremes of the Asians and Europeans, and partakes of their respective virtues. To be more specific, Turkish women are modern, educated and socially active, but modest and *pardah*-observing. In numerous public and private schools, they are taught, besides other substantive courses, French and, at some places, also music. They can get even technical education. Moreover, they have freedom of movement. They go out to markets and entertainment parks, and participate in parties and academic gatherings. Shiblī is particularly appreciative of Turkish women educationists and writers.[66]

This was Shiblī's first exposure to a semi-Western feminist culture in an Islamic society. And it remained his ideal until the very last. That was the ideal he searched in medieval, especially Indian, Islam,[67] and that was the ideal which he wanted realised among contemporary Indian Muslim women. That was partly the reason for his infatuation with 'Aṭīyyah Begam Fayḍī, and for his further encouragement to her in this direction.[68] It is a measure of Shiblī's liberal-mindedness in this regard that he was even willing to let

66. *Safarnāmah*, pp. 130 f.
67. *Maqālāt*, IV, 56, 60-63; V, 112.
68. *Khuṭūṭ*, *passim*.

'Aṭīyyah Begam attend a meeting of the Nadwat al-'Ulamā' and to let her elder sister, the Begam of Janjīrah, lay the foundation stone of the new building of Dār al-'Ulūm of Nadwah.[69] One may perhaps want to disregard these as exceptional cases, but one cannot ignore Shiblī's ideas on an adequate syllabus for women, which he expresses in his letters to 'Aṭīyyah Begam. In one of his letters he says:

> "I am totally against having a separate syllabus for women. This is a fundamental error into which even Europe is falling. Effort should be made to decrease the distance which has been created between the two sexes and not to increase it and let their respective manners, habits and tastes become disparate. If the divergence goes on increasing like this, both will eventually become two separate species. An American lady has written a nice book on this subject. . . . However, courses on child-nursing and-education, etc., should be added to women's syllabus."[70]

In another letter he writes:

> "You are of the opinion that women should study the worldly and economic sciences less [than men]. You do not like that women should earn their livelihood and sustain themselves. But remember that all the wrongs which men have done to women were on account of the fact that women were dependent on them . . . as long as women will continue to be frail, men will not give them their full rights."[71]

It is interesting to compare these radical ideas

69. Ibid., p. 108. 70. Ibid., pp. 46 f. 71. Ibid., p. 53.

of Shiblī with those of Sayyid Aḥmad Khān. The last mentioned was totally against imparting new education to women. His words are: "it is against my wish that you should start studying the presently current profane (*nāmubārak*) books instead of those holy books which your grandmothers have been reading."[72]

Above, we saw incidentally that Shiblī finds nothing objectionable in learning music, even by women.[73] The question of the lawfulness or otherwise of music did not seem to bother him at all. The same is true with regard to the pictures of living beings. He dares not publish a photo in *Al-Nadwah*,[74] but he is proud of the medieval Muslim contribution to painting.[75] He is aware of its prohibition in Islam, but is not worried at all by the fact. "We are not concerned with the religious dictum, but the historical fact is that the Muslims were not less advanced in this art," he says.[76] What is one supposed to make of these views? That Shiblī was knowingly flouting a precept of Islam? Hardly that, we would say. It would be

72. Sayyid Aḥmad Khān, *Mukammal Majmū'ah-i Laykcharz*, p. 251.

73 See above, p. 84. See also his letters to 'Aṭīyyah Begam Fayḍī, in which he encourages her in this direction. He himself claimed to be versed in the art. *Khuṭūṭ*, pp. 64-66, 93 f.

74. *Makātīb*, II, 217.

75. *Maqālāt*, IV, 96; *Makātīb*, I, 278.

76. *Maqālāt*, IV, 96; he not only let his own pictures taken, but was very pleased when a noted artist, indeed the husband of 'Aṭīyyah Begam, did a painting of his which won a prize in a Paris exhibition. *Makātīb*, I, 284 f.

more in line with his thinking, unless we have completely failed to understand Shiblī, to give to a practice legal validity of its own and prefer it to an ineffective precept. This also seems to go with his stand on *pardah* (in the sense of veil). Since it was a common practice, according to Shiblī, it cannot be done away with lightly. The only thing which can invalidate a practised precept is an urgent social need, examples of which we are going to see presently.

Shiblī not only agreed with Shāh 'Abd al-'Azīz's famous *fatwā* that India is *dār al-amn* and *ribā* is lawful in it, but also wrote an independent treatise on this subject in which he went one step further and argued that bank interest (*munāfa'*) is not usury (*sūd*).[77] Another, more telling example is that during the Balkan Wars Shiblī gave a *fatwā*, as perhaps did a few others, that, instead of sacrificing animals on the occasion of *'Īd al-Aḍḥā*, their price should be given in aid to the Turks. He went ahead and said that the latter has superiority (*afḍalīyyat*) over the former.[78] Last but not least, Shiblī made an earnest effort to prove that *waqf-i awlād* is an essential precept of Islam, and to have it enforced as a law by the government.[79] Why? Simply because the land-holding Muslim families were being ruined by the division

77. We could not get hold of this *risālah.* Probably it was never published. The statement made above is based on Sulaymān Nadwī's brief description of it. *Makātīb*, II, 165.

78. Ibid., I, 342 f.

79. *Maqālāt*, I, 81-102.

of inheritance into small units, not all of which fell to the lot of competent persons.[80] Very conveniently Shiblī forgot the basic law of inheritance of Islam which he had praised elsewhere, for quite the opposite reasons, as one of the most important socio-economic institutions of Islam.[81]

80. *Maqālāt-i Sar Sayyid*, V, 97.
81. *Al-Kalām*, pp. 161 ff.

III

Liberal Politics

(1)

As an introduction to Shiblī's political thinking we may as well begin with what his biographer says on the subject:

"In view of the attachment he had with Islam, Islamic civilisation, history, sciences and arts, it was only natural that he should hold dear the rule of Islam and should wish to see the picture he had been looking at in the books realised in actuality; and that, on the other hand, he should fully turn away from those rude hands which plucked out the flowers of the garden of Islam. His politics was precisely this."[1]

Avoid the temptation of imputing any idea of revivalism and pan-Islamism (Afghānī type) to it and there is no doubt that the fountainhead of Shiblī's politics, on an inter-Islamic level, was a sense of the community of Islam. The universality of the *millat*, he says in a verse, "extends over 'Irāq, Fāris, Najd, Ḥijāz and Qayrawān".[2] It was this sense of the community of Islam which made

1. Sayyid Sulaymān Nadwī, *Ḥayāt*, p. 585.
2. *Kullīyāt*, p. 59.

him, a British subject, take interest in the vicissitudes of the Ottoman Empire. And then it is perhaps also true that it was this inter-Islamic involvement which, however paradoxical it may seem, drove him to the politics of an entirely different nature in his own native land—the British of course providing the necessary bridge between the two.

Shiblī did not write extensively on the subject of contemporary Islamic or Indian politics. In fact, it is noteworthy that, except for a few articles, and a few references in his letters, all that Shiblī has written on politics is in poetry (though he is reported to have talked a lot about it in private meetings).[3] A considerable portion of his *Kullīyāt* consists of poems on political themes. This may be taken to indicate how great was the role of emotions in Shiblī's politics.[4] It was perhaps this excess of emotions in political matters which made Shiblī almost a romantic on the inter-Islamic level and, in a different sense, perhaps also in the Indian sphere.

(2)

Despite the fact that since after the 1857 up-

3. Sayyid Sulaymān Nadwī, op. cit., pp. 590, 609.

4. This is further corroborated by his own admission that "despite having composed thousand[s] of verses, I do not at all have command over poetical composition; that is, I cannot write a single word except under some special, sudden influence" (*Makātīb*, I, 308). Sulaymān Nadwī has also underlined this fact in his Foreword to Shiblī's *Kullīyāt* (pp. 1 f.).

rising India had come under the direct rule of the British Government, there was a considerable section of Indian Muslims who had recognised from some time in the past the Ottoman claim to the universal Islamic caliphate—a recognition which, though religious in nature, was not devoid of political implications. All was well as long as Britain itself pursued a pro-Ottoman policy and even encouraged this attitude among Indian Muslims. But with the manifest shift in British policy regarding the Ottomans, in the last decades of the nineteenth century, tension began to develop between the two loyalties.[5] Sayyid Aḥmad Khān reacted in the following manner:

> "We Muslims living in India are the subjects of the British Government . . . it is our religious duty to be well-wishing and loyal to the British Government . . . we are not the subjects of Sulṭān 'Abd al-Ḥamīd Khān, may God perpetuate his power, nor has he any kind of authority over us or our country. He neither is, nor can be, a caliph over us according to *sharī'ah* or religion. If he has any right to caliphate, then it is confined to his own country and to the Muslims living under his sway."[6]

This statement is typical of Sayyid Aḥmad Khān's stand in the matter during 1880's and 1890's.

To the great chagrin of his apologists, Shiblī also took precisely the same stand in this matter, as is indicated by his article, "Khilāfat," which

5. Aziz Ahmad, *Islamic Modernism*, pp. 123 f.
6. Sayyid Aḥmad Khān, *Ākhirī Maḍāmīn*, pp. 32 f.

appeared in 1899. Though the article is incomplete, the meaning is abundantly clear: submission to the Ottoman Caliphate is not a precept of religion, nor a fact of history, for the Muslims who are not living under the Turkish Sultanate.[7] As late as 1908, Shiblī wrote another article, "Musalmānon ko Ghayr Madhhab Ḥukūmat kā Maḥkūm ho kar kiyūn-kar Rahnā Chāhīye," in which he tried to show, on the basis of the Qur'ān, *Ḥadīth, fiqh* and history, that Muslims should remain loyal to whichever government they might have occasion to live under. In connection with this Shiblī cites the precedent of Naṣīr al-Dīn al-Ṭūsī who even destroyed Islam out of his loyalty to, Halākū; "though I do not like it," he adds. The article ends with a Persian couplet: "We have not read the story of Alexander and Darius; do not ask from me except the story of affection and loyalty."[8] Whether out of conviction or caution or both, Shiblī does not give the

7. *Maqālāt*, I, 179-84. Sulaymān Nadwī claims that Shiblī's views on the subject were different from that of Sayyid Aḥmad Khān (op cit., p. 587) He further claims that Shiblī did not write the article out of his own free will, but was made to write it Without disclosing the hidden hand behind this article, Nadwī merely offers the fact that it was left incomplete as an argument for its having been written under pressure (ibid., p. 631) At another place he offers still another defence: the article was descriptive, not prescriptive (ibid., p. 142).

8. *Maqālāt*, I, 165-71. Once again Sulaymān Nadwi felt the need to explain the article away and said, "this [the article] was as if the price paid for the annual grant of [Rs.] 6000 which it [the Government] had sanctioned for the Dār al-'Ulūm [of Nadwah]" (op. cit., p. 632).

slightest indication of any doubt as to the lawfulness of the subject status of Indian Muslims under the British Government and the invalidity of any political implications of the Ottoman claim in this respect. On this issue he and Sayyid Aḥmad Khān thought alike.

This did not, however, prevent Shiblī, as it did not prevent Sayyid Aḥmad Khān,[9] from wishing sincerely the consolidation and perpetuation of the government of their co-religionists, the Ottomans. One should note in this connection that in 1892 Shiblī visited Constantinople and a few other Egyptian and Syrian towns. Afterwards he wrote a *Safarnāmah* in which he praised many an educational and social institution of the Turkish Sultanate and made no attempt to hide his feelings for the Sulṭān.[10] Moreover, in 1896, he wrote a brief article on the Armenian Question. In this article Shiblī blamed the British for inciting the Armenians against the Turkish Government, showed the Porte's benevolent treatment of them and maintained that, contrary to the British news reports, Armenia was becoming pacified.[11]

The only difference between Shiblī and Sayyid Aḥmad Khān was that when there were occasions of conflict between the two loyalties, one political-concrete-British, the other religious-spectral-

9. Muḥammad Amīn Zubayrī, *Dhikr-i Shiblī*, pp. 48 f., 54 f.
10. See above, p. 84; see below, p. 95.
11. *Maqālāt*, VIII, 185-89.

Turkish, Shiblī, in his Islamic zeal, would sometimes forget the reality at home,[12] something which never happened in the case of Sayyid Aḥmad Khān.[13] However, on such occasions, when the storm of Shiblī's emotions subsided, he would try to make amends for his thoughtlessness.[14] Consequently, we find in his writings and behaviour until the end of his life evidence both for insolent and subdued postures towards the government.[15] Shiblī's protagonists and antagonists have gone to extremes on this subject. The former would have in Shiblī's thinking a level of political self-confidence and anti-Britishness which was not really there,[16] and which was characteristic only of a later phase of Indian-British relations. This, of course, necessitated far-fetched explanations of Shiblī's pro-government writings as well as of those amends which Shiblī would make with the government for his emotional outbursts.[17] The antagonists, on the other hand, accuse Shiblī of cowardice and sycophancy on the

12. Sayyid Sulaymān Nadwī, op. cit., p. 632.

13. This is an important point in order not only to understand the politics but also the respective characters of Shiblī and Sayyid Aḥmad Khān. Sayyid Aḥmad Khān was a very cool-headed man, who never crossed the self-imposed limits. Shiblī, on the other hand, was a very impulsive man, who hardly knew any rules. And yet, intrinsically, Sayyid Aḥmad Khān was a braver man and a better person than Shiblī—however much one may want to disagree with his politics.

14. Sayyid Sulayman Nadwī, op. cit., pp. 633 f.

15. Ibid., pp. 630-36.

16. Ibid., pp. 607 f.

17. Ibid., pp. 630-36.

basis of these writings.[18] These gentlemen tend to overlook the fact that it was unthinkable at that time, even for the Indian National Congress, to talk of disloyalty to the government. They should rather give credit to Shiblī, perhaps not a very courageous man at bottom, for being able to denounce the almighty British as much as he did in some of the testiest verses of Urdu.[19]

(3)

As mentioned earlier, Shiblī's interest and involvement in Muslim politics outside India—which to him was synonymous with the ups and downs in the fortunes of the Ottoman Sultanate—was based on his Islamic feelings. To him the Ottoman Sultanate was Islam personified, and the Sulṭān was its strength. This is evident from his report of Sulṭān 'Abd al-Ḥamīd's state-drive in Constantinople which Shiblī had visited in 1892. What is worth noticing in this description is the intensity of his feelings for the Sulṭān in whom he saw the political might of Islam.[20] Another example is his reaction to the news of the Ottoman Constitutional Revolution of 1908: "Muslims recalled the lesson of *amruhum shūrā* now. . . . 'Abd al-Ḥamīd atoned

18. Muḥammad Amīn Zubayrī, op. cit., pp. 34-37, 63, 140 f.; Shaykh Muḥammad Ikrām, *Shiblī Nāmah*, pp. 256 f.

19. *Kulliyāt*, pp. 53-56, 59, 79, 82-85, 101-03.

20. *Makātib*, I, 15 f.; *Safarnāmah*, pp. 112-17.

for the sins of Mu'āwiyah."[21]

Shiblī's attitude towards Ottoman Turkey was so romantic and emotionally based that he never tried or desired to know what was really happening inside the Empire. His view of the Armenian Question, mentioned before, is only one instance of it. Even the fact of the disintegration of the Empire could not bring the reality home: "Turkey nominally lost a few provinces. . . . These fragments will be regained after the rectification of internal conditions; the Young Turks know this point well."[22] When 'Aṭīyyah Begam Fayḍī visited Turkey a year after the Revolution and returned with the opinion that Turkey was a plaything of the Big Powers, and that the new loans had rendered it bankrupt, Shiblī would not believe it despite the facts that he had faith in 'Aṭīyyah's judgment in such matters, and that his trusted friend Mahdī Ḥasan also agreed with her.[23] How could anything possibly go wrong with this last bulwark of Islam?

With the Italian invasion of Tripoli in 1911 and the Balkan War in 1912, Shiblī's inter-Islamic political thinking, or emotion, was further crystallised. In a stirring poem filled with despair and appositely entitled "Shahr Āshob-i Islām" (Wasteland of Islam) he identified the Turkish defeat, which must have been a rude shock to

21. *Makātīb*, II, 218.
22. Ibid., II, 219.
23. Ibid., II, 220.

him, with the material and ideological decline of Islam. To him it looked like the beginning of the end. In a verse, he said: "Decline of Dawlat-i 'Uthmān is the decline of *shar'-o millat.*" In his eyes all the intricacies of European-Turkish politics were part of a continuing Crusade which might end up with the Christian occupation of the holy city of Mecca. In another verse he says: "How much will you take the revenge for the Ayyūbid victory from us; how long will you show us the scene of the Crusade."[24]

(4)

As pointed out in the beginning, it was this inter-Islamic politics which eventually involved Shiblī in the native Indian politics with an unprecedented intensity. Two verses which Shiblī wrote on the notorious incident of the Mosque of Kānpūr (13 August 1913)—in which many Muslims

24. *Kulliyāt*, pp. 53 f. One can observe his feelings expressed in several other poems which Shiblī wrote at the time. In "Sar Āghā Khān kā Turkon se Khiṭāb," written both in Urdu and Persian, Shiblī ridiculed Āghā Khān for advising the Turks that if they left Europe and retreated into Asia, they would be safe from the attacks of European Powers. In "Khayr Maqdam-i Dāktar Anṣārī," recited on the return of the Indian medical mission from Turkey, Shiblī praised the members of the mission for the service they had rendered to the Turkish warriors of faith out of their Islamic sentiment of brotherhood, and described the Turkish misery and Christian-European brutality. In "Turkon se Khiṭāb," Shiblī congratulates the Turks on their victory at Adrianople. In "Hastī-i Muslim kī Rahā'ī," Shiblī gives the lie to British claim of friendship with Muslims and disinvolvement in Turkish debacle (ibid., pp. 55-60).

were killed by police firing—indicate that in Shiblī's mind a tangible link existed between the tragedies of the Balkan and Kānpūr. He says:

> Are you asking about the nation of the Arabian Prophet,
> Why is it decreasing today in number and manifestation?
> Listen! those precious treasures are buried,
> Some in the dust of the Balkan, some in Kānpūr.[25]

Since we know that this is more or less the time when Shiblī showed a vigorous interest in Indian politics, we can surmise that the link was the British omnipresence. Shiblī must have thought that it is they who are at the back of all the troubles, at home and abroad. It is time something should be done about it. Someone should ask: "O teachers of human civilisation! how long these atrocities? how long these horrors?"[26] Shiblī was not the only Muslim who took a lively interest in Indian politics around this time and the tragedies of the Balkan and Kānpūr were not the only reasons for it. (Even the loyal Aligarh was having second thoughts and the annulment of the partition of Bengal was also agitating the Muslim mind.)[27] Yet perhaps among his Muslim contem-

25. Ibid., p. 81. 26. Ibid., p. 53.

27. In 1911, on the occasion of the annulment of the partition of Bengal, Wiqār al-Mulk wrote an article, "Hindostān men Musalmānon kī Ā'indah Ḥālat" in the *Aligarh Institute Gazette*. The following extract will give an idea of its tone: "This is now clear like midday sun that after having observed the present events it is useless to advise Muslims to bank upon the government. Time has passed for such trusts. The thing in which we should place our confidence, next

poraries in North-Western India Shiblī alone had the distinction of showing independence of mind and maturity of thought concerning national politics.

Politics in India began, in a real sense, with the establishment of the Indian National Congress in 1885. And in a speech on 28 December 1887, Sayyid Aḥmad Khān advised the Muslims against joining it. Evidence concerning Shiblī's reaction to Sayyid Aḥmad Khān's policy and his early attitude towards the Congress is contradictory.[28] This much, however, seems clear that if he conformed with it in the beginning, Shiblī

to the grace of God, is our own strength. The precedent of this presented by our compatriots [Hindus] is before our eyes" (Muḥammnd Amīn Zubayrī, *Tadhkirah-i Wiqār*, p. 341).

28. Maftūn Aḥmad says that he saw a letter which Mahdī Ḥasan, Shiblī's younger brother, wrote to Shiblī from Cambridge England, on 29 March 1888. It said : "I learnt from 'Abd al-Ra'ūf's letter that you are against that Congress which calls itself National Congress ... perhaps this is the first time that we are in agreement. Most of the Indians in England are in favour of this Congress The first to oppose it [here] is your younger brother, Mahdī" (*Adīb*, p. 61). This is the only direct evidence we have in favour of Shiblī's agreement with Sayyid Aḥmad Khān's Congress policy, at least in the beginning. There are several against it. In a letter of his, dated 23 December 1912, Shiblī himself claims that "For sixteen years I was with Sir Sayyid but in matters political I always differed with him, liked the Congress and often had arguments with Sir Sayyid" (*Ma'ārif*, XIV, 394). Khwājah Ghulām al-Thaqalayn writes in a note on Shibli's death : "Since the days of his professorship at the College, Mawlānā Shiblī had a great dislike for Sir Sayyid's political ideas" (Sayyid Sulaymān Nadwī, op. cit., p. 608). According to H.R.K. Sherwānī, one of the reasons of Shiblī's disappointment with Aligarh was the difference in political opinions; Shiblī had become a supporter of the new movement [Congress] (ibid., p. 798).

gradually moved away from Sayyid Aḥmad Khān's position to a more and more pro-Congress stance. As early as 1892 we have an indication of his democratic leanings.[29] In 1895 he was publicly disowning Sayyid Aḥmad's policy towards the Congress.[30] Sometime before March 1897, he perhaps wrote an article in *Aligarh Institute Gazette* under a pseudonym advising Muslim leaders to join the Congress.[31] By the turn of the century we find him subscribing to a pro-Congress newspaper.[32] It was not, however, before another decade in 1912 that Shiblī's ideas on Indian politics found a powerful expression in "Musalmānon kī Politikal Karvat".[33]

If the maturity of his ideas in this article is indicative of sustained thinking over a period of time, the timing is also very significant. It is

29. Ibid., p. 160. 30. *Maqālāt-i Yawm-i Shiblī*, p. 103.

31. Ibid. We could not find any such letter or article in the few issues of the *Gazette* available in the library of the Institute of Islamic Studies, McGill. There is, however, an article by Theodore Beck in answer to an 'Āzād', obviously a pseudonym, who had written an article in the *M.A.O. College Magazine* supporting the Congress. The issue containing the latter article is missing; but a few statements referred to by Beck are: Muslims gained nothing by keeping away from the Congress; on the contrary, they were harmed; the Congress will certainly succeed in its efforts one day or another; the Muslim leaders should join hands with the founders of the Congress; the way things are developing they will certainly result in the victory of representative government against personal rule; foreigners cannot understand the wishes and needs of a people better than the natives themselves. *Muhammadan Anglo-Oriental College Magazine*, V, 124, 128 f., 131.

32. Sayyid Sulaymān Nadwī, op. cit., p. 609.

33. *Maqālāt*, VIII, 148-84.

quite possible that Shiblī had done his thinking on Indian Muslim politics in its own right and had drawn his conclusion in favour of Muslim participation in the Congress in a purely Indian context. Also, one cannot deny that had there been no extra-Indian Islamic relevance, he still might have reacted in the same way and written the article in consequence of the annulment of the partition of Bengal, which took place in **1911**. But the indications are, as pointed out earlier, that Shiblī definitely got a psychological push from what had recently happened, and had been happening for some time in the past, to Turkey with the connivance and even instigation of the British.[34]

(5)

"Musalmānon kī Politikal Karvat," which Shiblī aptly describes as the prose commentary on his political poems,[35] is perhaps one of the most trenchant historical documents of the beginning of modern Muslim political consciousness in North-

34 Cf W.C. Smith, *Modern Islam in India*, pp. 233 f. The psychological significance of the Indian Muslim involvement in the pan-Islamic movement between 1870 and 1924 lay, according to Aziz Ahmad, "partly in relation to a feeling of insecurity in the midst of Hindu majority" (op. cit., p. 123). But it would seem that at least in Shiblī's case it was the other way round. It was the frustration on pan-Islamic front that had him running in search of security right in the midst of Hindu majority.

35. *Makātib*, I, 243.

Western India. It is not merely one of the early expressions of the discontent of North-Western Indian Muslims with the policy they had been faithfully pursuing *vis a vis* the British Government since the days of Sayyid Aḥmad Khān. It is perhaps also—together with Wiqār al-Mulk's "Hindostān men Musalmānon kī Ā'indah Ḥālat"[36] —a pioneering document which helped in giving form to the political discontent of Indian Muslims and contributed in setting the trend and the tone of their future political behaviour.[37] Here its resemblance with Wiqār al-Mulk's article ends. While Wiqār al-Mulk still pursued the policy of Hindu-Muslim separatism,[38] Shiblī boldly set forth the more progressive course of Hindu-Muslim political unity. It is deplorable that Shiblī's article was almost never given its due historical importance, perhaps because of two factors: one, he became a victim of pro-Aligarh and pro-Pakistan belligerency; two, he was overshadowed by later, more loquacious Indian Muslim leaders like Muḥammad 'Alī and Abū al-Kalām. For us the article is significant in that it throws light on still another aspect of the modern liberal content of Shiblī's thought. It is in the context of his attempt to forcefully circumvent the communal

36. See above, ref. 27.

37. Ṭufayl Aḥmad Manglorī, *Musalmānon kā Roshan Mustaqbil*, pp. 374-79. Sayyid Sulayman Nadwī, op. cit., pp. 621 f.

38. Muḥammad Amīn Zubayrī, *Tadhkirah-i Wiqār*, pp. 341 ff.

tendencies among the Muslims and to make a strong case for joint Hindu-Muslim political action that Shiblī's thinking about two important concepts or institutions of modern polity, democracy and nationalism, also comes into relief, though he never refers to them by their names. But in the first place Shiblī is concerned about the deeply implanted Muslim loyalism towards the British in his part of the country. This loyalist attitude is tantamount to political inactivity and also leads to communalism. To be politically active is to act *like* and *with* the Hindus. Shiblī is fully aware, even highly appreciative, of the fact that his Hindu compatriots were far ahead of Muslims in political consciousness, vision, initiative, struggle, boldness, sacrifice, dedicated leadership and, consequently, achievements. (The recent Reform Scheme, which laid the foundation of self-government, was the crowning proof of this fact.) What Muslims could not get by begging from the government—and they did not even ask for much —Hindus got that plus much more by pressuring the government.[39] Even the Muslims in other parts of the country did not remain unaffected by this struggle. (Instances are: Badr al-Dīn Ṭayyibjī and Raḥmat Allāh Sayānī in Bombay, Sayyid Muḥammad in Madras and Ameer Ali in Calcutta.)[40]

39. *Maqālāt*, VIII, 149-51, 154, 164, 166, 168-70.
40. Ibid., p. 154.

"But it is a matter of great surprise that the [area comprising] western and northern provinces and Agra, Delhi and the Punjab—which had once been the centre of the government and the heart and brain of India, where Muslims had received more education as compared to other parts of India, and where the scions of the best families of the Arabs and the 'Ajams were present—remained so insensitive to the politics that even now it stammers in uttering the word 'politics'."[41]

According to Shiblī, the reason for the political backwardness of Muslims of this area is that, through Sayyid Aḥmad Khān, they were kept away from politics—from legitimate freedom and seeking their rights.[42]

"The thing which we took to be politics [Shiblī says] was an insult to politics. Our politics whose voice fell into our ears, like *Kalimah-i Shahādat*, since the day of birth was only this: 'the time has not yet arrived; right now we should make ourselves fit for politics; only education is needed now; our numbers are small, therefore, representative government is not suitable for us'. These words were repeated so many times that they fused into the anatomy of the nation . . . when the word politics is mentioned in the midst of the general body of Muslims, one is astounded to see that the best educated young man repeats them like a gramophone."[43]

Consequently, Muslim political consciousness became absolutely dead. In contrast to the Hindus who made great sacrifices for national uplift, the

41. Ibid., pp. 154 f. See W. C. Smith, op. cit., pp. 195 ff., for an analysis of this situation.

42. *Maqālāt*, VIII, 155.

43. Ibid., VIII, 149-51.

Muslims made "B.A. and jobs" their ideal. This base motive turned the Muslim into a nation of timids and cowards. "Our politicial dictionary defined legitimate freedom as rebellion." A Parsee or Hindu joins the Congress, criticises the government and still remains the member of the Parliament and of the Viceroy's Council. But Muslims are afraid to participate in the Muhammadan Educational Conference, and Sayyid Aḥmad Khān has to declare that it is not forbidden to participate in it. "We know that many an honoured gentleman made their membership of the Muslim League dependent upon the permission from Ṣāḥib Kaliktar Bahādur."[44]

Muslims did not pay any attention to politics in the first place. But when they suddenly decided otherwise, they came up with the Muslim League. "What is this unusual creature? Is it politics? God forbid, no. Is it anti-Congress? No. Is it a House of Lords? Yes, the masquerade seems somewhat like that."[45] Shiblī calls the Muslim League by various other names,[46] insinuates its government origin and insists that it "cannot become politics today or a thousand years after".[47]

Why is it that Shiblī refuses to regard the kind of politics the Muslim League was engaged in as

44. Ibid., VIII, 150 f. 45. Ibid., VIII, 161.

46. "A spurious, useless thing," "mirage," "political Thespians," "children's play". Ibid., VIII, 163, 168, 171.

47. Ibid., VIII, 163 f.

genuine? Because politics, according to Shiblī, is born with the recognition of the principle that the British Government is a parliamentary (constitutional) government. This, Shiblī says:

"means that the subjects have every kind of say in the administration, have the right to express opinion and to criticise. Indeed, it is more true to say that the subjects themselves are the ruled and the rulers; they make law for themselves and act upon it."

There is no confusion in this matter as far as England is concerned. But in India its course alters

"and that is the point from which the line of our, that is Indian, politics begins."[48]

What Shiblī means is that self-government (under British protection) should be the aim of Indian politics. Until that aim is achieved, "politics is the name of the mutual demands of the government and the subjects, and not of the subjects' quarrels with, and demands from, each other."[49] In other words, Shiblī would have Hindus and Muslims jointly struggle for greater participation in the government of India, rather than fight with each other.

In Shiblī's searching analysis, the Muslim League falls ridiculously short of this standard. Shiblī regards the Simla Deputation as the foundation-stone and the continuing spirit of the

48. Ibid., VIII, 152. 49. Ibid., VIII, 165.

Muslim League, calls it "the biggest play (*tamāshā*) staged on the national stage" and characterises its aim in these terms: out of those national rights which Hindus have achieved through their thirty years' struggle, a part should be earmarked for the Muslims. All that the Muslim League stands for is, in Shiblī's view, that "Hindus are over-dominating us; therefore, we should protect ourselves". The rest is face-saving and local colour [50] Shiblī compares the respective demands of the Congress and the League, and shows the pettiness of the latter, and maintains that if the Congress' demands are met, it will change the destiny of India. He also criticises the League for inefficiency in its methods, incompetence of its representatives, want of seriousness of purpose, lack of selflessness and sacrifice and finally for its moneyed, landed or knighted and, therefore, interest-bound and slavish leadership. Shiblī derides the Muslim League's financial dependence on a certain "generous hand" (meaning probably the Āghā Khān) which controls its policies.[51]

Despite his utter disgust with its aims, methods and leaders, Shiblī seems to accept the Muslim League as an accomplished fact of political life and would like to see it reformed and function, if it stands for Muslim political activism, like another political party in addition to the Congress. (The presence of liberal, conservative and

50. Ibid., VIII, 164.

51. Ibid., VIII, 165-71.

radical schools or groups in the politics of England can serve as a model.)[52] He even makes certain suggestions for this purpose of which the following are very significant in order to understand the drift of his mind. The League should give up its communal stance and think in terms of India. For instance, it should press for Permanent Settlement. "Suppose," he says, "if, like Bengal, in our part of the country too *Istimrārī Band-o Bast* comes to be, will this be a blessing for India, or only that a few more Muslims get jobs?" The demand should be made for the participation of Indians in all administrative affairs. In short, except for any particular resolution, the Muslim League should include all the proposals of the Congress in its programme and should fight for them legally like the Hindu moderate group. Ameer Ali's recent proposal for a joint Hindu-Muslim stage for common problems should be adopted. The Muslim League executive committee should be rid of big land-owners.[53]

(Shiblī had very definite views on the question of political leadership. He elaborates upon them in a separate article entitled "Līdaron kā Quṣūr hay yā Līdar banāne wālon kā?"[54] To him the office of a leader is different from that of a benefactor and should be clearly distinguished. Thus the Āghā Khān is our benefactor for his very generous con-

52. Ibid., VIII, 158 f., 178.
53. Ibid., VIII, 171-73.
54. Ibid., VIII, 182 ff.

tributions to the Aligarh University. But the person needed for leadership is one "who is free, like Gokhale, from title, property, wealth and all other ties; is zealous, bold and, at the same time, an expert in politics and a long-time student of political literature". If such persons are not found in the nation, Shiblī would rather keep the post vacant and wait.)[55]

(6)

At one point Shiblī went so far as to concede that the Congress, not necessarily exhaustive of the possibilities of political expression, "is not advantageous to us" and that "our needs, if common with, are also different from those of the Hindus and we therefore need a separate political stage".[56] But the Muslim League could not come up to his idea of that separate political stage, and, despite his promise to stop opposing it subject to its being reformed,[57] he remained sceptical about its role in Indian politics. The League continued to be anathema for him till the very last. The fact was that he never really accepted it in his heart. And this was not merely because it failed to correct itself radically enough for Shiblī's

55. Ibid., VIII, 183 f.

56. Ibid., VIII, 158 f., 161. This concession on the part of Shiblī appears to be more methodological than real. He is trying to talk the Muslims into taking up aggressive, demanding politics.

57. Ibid., VIII, 178.

liking (he would not be satisfied with anything short of a virtual Congressisation of the Muslim League) and on that score went on incurring his scathing critcism.[58] A further, more basic, reason for Shiblī's almost total rejection of the League was that he could not stomach the very rationale offered for a separate political platform for the Muslims. He criticised Wiqār al-Mulk's aforementioned article in the following, revealing words:

"[It] could have been the voice of a truly courageous Muslim, had it not contained this incorrect logic that, if we join the National Congress, our existence will be destroyed in the same way in which small rivers vanish into the ocean. If the Parsees numbering only one hundred thousand can preserve their existence in the midst of one hundred and ninety million Hindus and fifty million Muslims, then fifty million Muslims should not be afraid that their existence will be destroyed."[59]

Shiblī, who had no way of knowing that India would eventually be partitioned on communal basis, accepted it as a fact that "Muslims are a minority now and will remain a minority always,"[60] and still had the courage to believe that the Muslims can and should make a joint political platform with the Hindus. What he did not believe, or at least pretended not to believe, was, again, the rationale offered by a Muslim correspondent of the *Pioneer* that "since it is now

58. *Kullīyāt*, pp. 67-71, 104-06, 108.
59. *Maqālāt*, VIII, 149. 60. Ibid., VIII, 157.

obvious that because of the weakening of Turkey and Iran our foreign status will not be the same, therefore, we should join up with the Hindus."[61] Shiblī, on the other hand, maintained that

"it is good to join up with the Hindus; but, then, it was always good and will always be good. The new need which the correspondent had mentioned is a disgrace for Islam. Should we take refuge with neighbours because we do not have a support any longer? Could Turkey and Iran, were they strong, have helped us against our neighbours? Did the British believe in Simla Deputation's boast that our political weight is more than that of our neighbours?"[62]

Shiblī puts the main blame for Hindu-Muslim disunity on Muslim shoulders—on the Muslims' quarrelsomeness, and their deliberate provocation of communal feelings for selfish ends.[63] Shiblī became so self-critical here as to say that "it is obvious that the Hindus never marched against Iran and Arabia. It is we who invaded their country and destroyed their famous temple Somnath and others in Banāras and Mathrā." But for all that the Hindus have been in the past and still are very forgiving, generous and helpful to the Muslims.[64]

61. Ibid., VIII, 141; quoted by Shiblī.

62. Ibid.

63. Ibid., VIII, 173 f.

64. Ibid., VIII, 174 ff. In his description of Hindu magnanimity and cooperation with Muslims, Shiblī apparently became so one-sided that it hurt the Muslim feeling. He had to write a sort of postscript showing that the Hindus were not being friendly with the Muslims for nothing. What the Hindus did was in response to the nice and benevolent treatment of them by the Muslim conquerors once they had settled down in India. Ibid., VIII, 178-81.

(7)

In the light of the above it would not be difficult to comprehend that Shiblī was deeply impressed by the aims and methods of the moderate group in the Congress led by Gokhale, and that he regarded parliamentary democracy as an ideal for India. He was, in short, a liberal and a democrat in Indian politics.[65] Shiblī does not explain why it is good to establish common political bonds with the Hindus, religiously. Perhaps the question did not occur to him as such. And if it did, he perhaps refused to regard it a religious question. We do not find him concerned with this question in the manner of, say, Āzād, Madanī, Iqbāl or Mawdūdī. Apparently the only authority that Shiblī looked for, and managed to find, was in historical precedents of Indian (not even early, Arabian) Islam.[66] One may perhaps justifiably characterise his whole approach in this matter as areligious or secular. This is borne out by more positive evidence from none other than Shiblī himself. According to his own statement, the Indian Muslims have two statuses: one, that they are the subjects of the British Government; two, that they are Muslims. Shiblī insists that in politics the former has pre-

65. It is interesting to note that he also comes out strongly against anarchism and nihilism and would like to maintain the levels in society. *Al-Kalām*, p. 237. But as compared to Sayyid Aḥmad Khān he has adjusted himself to the fact that persons of lowly origin may rise to high positions. *Maqālāt*, VIII, 158.

66. *Maqālāt*, VIII, 174-81.

cedence over the later.[67] Indeed, at one place he goes so far as to suggest by implication that religion and politics are no longer combined as they were in medieval times.[68] Although made as a statement of fact, its message is unmistakable, particularly if seen in conjunction with Shiblī's concept of Islam as a religion, described elsewhere in this thesis.[69] After that it becomes easier to understand how he could afford to be so uninhibited a liberal in politics and why he was such an unconditional supporter of the Congress and the Hindu-Muslim unity. Shiblī's conception of the goodness of Hindu-Muslim political alliance does not seem to be merely tactical or temporary either. It may have been contingent in its origin, but it appears to have taken on the quality of a conviction.

In Shiblī's ideas on the subject of Hindu-Muslim unity and in his readiness to go to great lengths in this matter, we also find the early beginnings of the nationalist Islam or ***muttaḥiddah qawmīyyat*** (composite/united Indian nationalism) which was to be developed later into a full-fledged ideology by persons like Abū al-Kalām Āzād and Ḥusayn Aḥmad Madanī, who at the same time turned it into a theological proposition, something which Shiblī never did. To Shiblī it seemed just the right or the most obvious thing to do. He was

67. Ibid., VIII, 151 f.
68. Ibid., VIII, 179.
69. See above, p. 76.

a nationalist and he was a Muslim. But it is difficult to say what kind of nationalist Muslim he was. He is hard to categorise in terms of the various types of nationalist Muslims mentioned by Smith.[70] But if one has to squeeze him into one of them, then one should say that Shiblī is nearer in his nationalism, as in his democratic liberalism, to that brand of pro-Congress Muslim leaders a typical representative of which was Badr al-Dīn Ṭayyibjī of Bombay. Indeed, one may usefully recall here that Shiblī, in the post-Aligarh phase of his life, was almost a regular visitor to Bombay, in fact to the very house (of 'Aṭīyyah Begam Fayḍī) to which Ṭayyibjī was closely related by blood and in ideas.[71] One may, therefore, reasonably infer that Shiblī was influenced in his nationalist thinking by the progressive Muslim school of politics of Bombay, a counterpart of the Madras and Calcutta schools.

Finally, it should also be pointed out that Shiblī's nationalism was typically without bark or bite. His was not what Smith would call "negative" nationalism.[72] He did not share the views of the extremist group of the Congress led by Tilak. He had no intention to oust the British from India and win *swarāj* or *āzādī*. One wonders if he ever visualised such a possibility. All he

70. W. C. Smith, op. cit., pp. 251 ff.
71. *Adīb*, p. 305 ; Shaykh Muḥammad Ikrām, op. cit., p. 220.
72. W.C. Smith, *Islam in Modern History*, pp. 79 ff.

wanted was to contain the British constitutionally with the fullest possible cooperation of the Hindu compatriots and also reap the fruits together with them. Perhaps this was his way of getting even with the British!

Thus, Shiblī may be a romantic when it came to extra-Indian Islam or Islamic past, but he was a realist in contemporary Indian politics; or was he really, now that the British are out and the children of Mother India are divided into two political units?

Conclusion

In conclusion, it appears that Shiblī was willing to sacrifice, as far as it was feasible, the traditional form of Islam for the modern fact of Islam. Herein he is hardlydistinguishable from Sayyid Aḥmad Khān. Both were in favour of change in the religion which they had inherited from the past. Both were basically responding to the challenges of Europe's scientific outlook. Both cherished the desire to preserve Islam in some form or the other. The difference arises in respect of the nature or extent of the change they were ready to accept in their faith, or, in other words, with regard to their respective conclusions about Islam as a religion. Sayyid Aḥmad Khān would reduce Islaṃ to a form of deism or natural religion, the essence of which is "truth rather than faith" and "Truth, in so far as it is cognizable by human reason, is identified with nature and its laws." Sayyid Aḥmad's thesis, if accepted, would not only have compromised the individuality and specificity of the Islamic faith, but would also have robbed it of its vitality, rendering it static, cold and bloodless, and converting it almost into a mechanical formula. Eventually, it would have killed Islam as a living, vibrating, emotionally-satisfying faith. Sayyid Aḥmad Khān's Islam was too negative to be held in heart. In his attempt to save Islam from annihilation by divesting it of its unnatural and unscientific elements, perhaps unknowingly, Sayyid Aḥmad Khān had deprived it also of its human and divine elements. Perhaps that partly explains why Sayyid Aḥmad Khān's conception of Islam could not gain sympathy and success. On the other hand, Shiblī's conception of Islam became "popular," even if only relatively. This is borne out by the casual fact that the Library of the University of Karachi holds twelve copies of *Al Kalām* pretty worn out from frequent use, while Sayyid Aḥmad Khān's *tafsīr* or his theological articles, far from being consulted, have not even been duplicated.

Shiblī's Islam was comparatively a thing of flesh and blood, a living organism. It seemed at once human and—or rather therefore—theopneustic. The fact that in the end Shiblī inclined towards Rūmī's concept of *waḥdat al-wujūd* merely shows that Shiblī was not a systematic thinker. It did not go with the main thrust of his theological thinking. Shiblī wanted to keep intact the idea of revelation from a living, active and personal God to an essentially responsible and actively responding mankind. He endorsed the universal quality of revelation, but at the same time believed in special revelation to Prophets in general and the Prophet of Islam in particular. He saw to it that the mode and message of revelation conformed to nature, science and, above all, to reason, but he would not have it circumscribed, determined or created at least by science or nature. To him Islam was a self-necessitating and self-justifying process of faith and action, even if not a self-explaining and self-relating one. This is what makes him an Islamic modernist in the truer and more profound sense of the word. He would change the face but not the faith of Islam as something spiritual and moral in its essence. This is all the more evident from his attitude towards law and politics.

While it would not be fair to suggest that Shiblī was deliberately whittling away what he held to be the sacred law of Islam or to suspect his religious and intellectual integrity, it should be admitted that he was in favour of fairly radical changes in the medieval law of Islam through a major reshuffle and redefinition of the traditional bases of Islamic law-making. This would certainly result in altering the conventional picture of the *sharī'ah* and, perhaps more significantly, would also render it resilient enough to absorb the subsequent shocks of socio-historical upheavals. Indeed, the results were so sweeping that they would have surprised Shiblī if he had pursued them to their logical end. For this reason, or due to lack of systematic thinking, Shiblī makes no attempt to spell out the full implications of his legal ideas, or to present a coherent picture of the *sharī'ah* for modern times. Or was it because Shiblī realised that being too logical, explicit or comprehensive in the matters of a divine-cum-human *sharī'ah* would prove to be self-defeating, and inhibit that freedom of interaction between the human and the divine in history which was, or should be, the hall-mark of an ever-evolving *sharī'ah*? Be that as it may, the fact remains that Shiblī was in favour, not only of changing the positive contents of Islamic law, but also of releasing its potential for further changes.

The same liberal spirit is manifest in Shiblī's approach to politics, which is even more radical than his approach to law. Indeed, at a superficial glance he seems to be almost indifferent to religious considerations in politics. This view is particularly strengthened by the fact that Shiblī chose to be secular and nationalist in politics. But, in our opinion, this should not be understood to mean that Shiblī took his Islam rather lightly. On the contrary, we believe that his decision to become areligious in politics was a serious religious decision, which would have been made impossible without his specific view of Islam as essentially comprising beliefs, rituals and morals. While it would not be true to assert that Shiblī deduced his nationalistic ardour from any positive interpretation of Islam as recommending loyalty to, and concern for, a society transcending the bounds of Islam, it would be equally untrue to hold that Shiblī was a nationalist in spite of being a Muslim. He did work out, even if implicitly, a relation between the two facts. Only he reached the conclusion that the two facts were unrelated, or should be kept unrelated, to one another in the modern, multi-communal polity of India. Shiblī's conception of Islam was no hindrance to this. Indeed, it may even have been a positive source of inspiration. This would not preclude him from conceiving Islam and politics in a closer relationship in different situation, time and place.

When all was said and done, Islam still remained the primary concern and final frame of reference for Shiblī. It will be great injustice to him to think that he had gone overboard or changed his loyalties. He was a true forerunner of the breed of Islamic modernists typified by Fazlur Rahman whose *Islam* comes in the direct line of Shiblī's religious writings.

THE END

Appendix

A Chronological Bio-Bibliography of Shibli

1857-1863

Muḥammad Shiblī born to an upper middle-class, land-owning, Rājpūt family of Azamgarh, U.P. In addition to being a *zamīndār*, Shiblī's father was also a *tājir* and a *wakīl*. Shiblī was reported a precocious child.

1863-1876

Formal education began at the age of six. Learnt Qur'ān and Persian. Later studied Persian poetry and *ma'qūlāt* under Mawlānā Fārūq Charīyākotī, Islamic jurisprudence under Mawlānā Irshād Ḥusayn Rāmpūrī (both *ghālī* Ḥanafites; Shiblī's *nisbah*, Nu'mānī, result of this influence) and Arabic literature under Mawlānā Fayḍ al-Ḥasan, Professor in Oriental College, Lahore, taking especial interest in pre-Islamic Arabic poetry and memorising *Ḥamāsah*. Wrote *Ẓill al-Ghamām fī Mas'alat al-Qir'at Khalf al-Imām* (1875). Performed *Ḥajj*.

1876-1883

Shiblī's father made him study law; could pass the examination only in the second attempt. Tried his hand at practising law and a couple of official jobs in the local court of law, but failed to make a career out of them. For a while looked after his father's landed and business interests; but most of the time busy in general reading, poetry composition and disputing with the *ghayr muqal-*

lidīn. Wrote *Iskāt al-Mu'tadī 'alā Inṣāt al-Muqtadī* (1881).

1883-1898

Appointed Professor of Persian at the M.A.O College, Aligarh. Stayed close to Sayyid Aḥmad Khān and his library. Wrote two long poems: "Qaṣīdah-i 'Īdīyyah" (1883) and "Mathnawī Ṣubḥ-i Ummīd" (1884) to rouse the Indian Muslims and rally them round the Aligarh movement. Founded a modern type school for education in his native town and named it National School. Wrote his first research article "Musalmānon kī Guzashtah Ta'līm" (1886) and *Al-Ma'mūn* (1887). Wrote several historical articles such as "Jizyah," "Ḥuqūq al-Dhimmīyyīn," "Islāmī Kutubkhāne," "Kutubkhānah-i Iskandarīyah," etc., for the *Aligarh College Magazine* (1887-1892). Wrote *Sīrat al-Nu'mān* (1889-1890). Travelled to Turkey, Syria and Egypt for educational purposes and to search material for his books, especially *Al-Fārūq*; visited educational institutions, libraries, museums, teachers and scholars including 'Abduh; studied the syllabi of the modern and traditional educational institutions, which proved useful when he had to prepare the syllabi for certain educational institutions in his own country; was awarded Tamghah-i Majīdī by the Turkish Government. Upon his return, wrote *Sarfarnāmah-i Rūm-o Miṣr-o Shām* (1893) Government of India awarded the title of Shams al-'Ulamā'. Was appointed Fellow of Allahabad University and Member of its Faculty of Arts and Board of Studies. Wrote *Al-Fārūq* (1894-1898). Through Aligarh, he came to know many a distinguished people of his time (such as Muḥsin al-Mulk, Ḥālī, Nadhīr Aḥmad, 'Abd al-Razzāq Kānpurī and the Bilgirāmī Brothers, Sayyid 'Alī and Sayyid Ḥusayn) and became generally well known himself. Perhaps next to Sayyid Aḥmad Khān, he was on closest friendly terms with T.W. Arnold, Professor of Philosophy at Aligarh College; very frequently they met, exchanged ideas and their respective knowledge of Arabic and French. Muḥammad 'Alī and Ẓafar 'Alī Khān were two of his more prominent students who, by their own admission, were deeply influenced by him. Started taking increasing interest in Nadwat al-'Ulamā'. Resigned from Aligarh College after Sayyid Aḥmad Khan's death. Reasons for resignation became subject of a big controversy.

1898-1901

Multifarious activities and intermittent spells of illness. Looked after the earlier founded National School in Azamgarh; and put together his personal library there. Visited various places such as Allahabad, Lucknow, Kashmir, etc. Intended to attend the Orientalists' conference at Rome in 1899. Also wanted to go to Iran. Family troubles after the second marriage and father's death who bequeathed considerable financial obligations. Declined Arnold's invitation to come to Lahore, and went to Hyderabad instead.

1901-1905

Appointed *Nāẓim* of Sar Rishtah-i 'Ulūm-o Funūn in Hyderabad State. Participated in various literary meetings; and associated with Dāgh, Sharar, the Bilgirāmī Brothers and other literary figures. Wrote *Al-Ghazālī* and *'Ilm al-Kalām* (1902), *Al-Kalām* and *Mawāzinah-i Anis-o Dabīr* (1903), and *Sawāniḥ Mawlawī Rūm* (1904). Resigned from his job and left Hyderabad apparently due to local politics. Earlier, declined Muḥsin al-Mulk's offer to rejoin the Aligarh College.

1905-1913

Became Secretary of the Dār al-'Ulūm, Nadwat al-'Ulamā', Lucknow, and launched it on its new, more vigorous career; and himself embarked upon the most hectic and many-sided career of his life, at once educational, romantic and political. Expanded the membership and patronage of the Nadwah, raised funds and had the permanent building of the Dār al-'Ulūm constructed; effected important changes in the syllabus, method of education and the teaching personnel; took a select few of his students (such as Sayyid Sulaymān, 'Abd al-Salām and, for a short while, Abū al-Kalām) under his wing and groomed them for scholarship; held an educational fair under the auspices of Nadwah at Banāras; invited dignitaries like the Āghā Khān and Rashīd Riḍā' as chief guests to annual convocations. *Al-Nadwah*, the official organ of Nadwat al-'Ulamā', placed under Shiblī's editorship since 1904, now became the chief vehicle of his research and review articles, which constitute the major portion of the eight volumes of his *Maqālāt*. At Muḥammad 'Alī's request wrote a series of articles on Awrangzeb (1906-1908) Wrote *Shi'r al-'Ajam* in five volumes (1908-1912), winning a prize for it from the University of the Panjab as the best book of the year. Was persuaded by Muḥammad 'Alī to write a rebuttal to Margoliouth's work on the Prophet; started work on it in 1912. In a visit to Bombay met the Fayḍī Sisters and cultivated an enduring relationship especially with 'Aṭīyyah Begam; after losing a leg in an accident, visits to Bombay became frequent for the purpose of treatment, change of climate and also to see 'Aṭīyyah Begam; composed a series of love-poems collected under the titles *Dastah-i Gul* (1906-1907), and *Bū'e Gul* (1908); wrote interesting letters to 'Aṭīyyah Begam (1906-1909) compiled in *Khuṭūṭ-i Shiblī*. Also composed a great many Islamic and political poems (1911-1913) included in *Kullīyāt*; wrote his famous article "Musalmānon kī Polītikal Karwat" (1912). Despite his earnest desire to work in and through *'ulamā'*, Shiblī could not win them to his point of view and the Nadwah became a hotbed of controversies; on the question of the syllabus for the Dār al-'Ulūm and certain articles in *Al-Nadwah*, especially "Mas'alah-i Irtiqā' awr Darwin," was opposed by the *mawlawīs*; was condemned for his liberal ways; and branded *kāfir* on the basis of certain passages of *Al-Kalām*. Resigned.

1913-1914

Returned to Azamgarh and founded Dār al-Muṣannifīn, dedicating his house and his library to it; engaged himself in writing *Sīrat ul-Nabī*, and training specialists in various branches of Islamic learning. Died and was buried in Azamgarh.

Bibliography

Ahmad, Aziz, *Islamic Modernism in India and Pakistan, 1857-1964*, Oxford, 1967

Amīn, Qāsim Bak, *Musalmān 'Awrat kī Āzādī*, Tr. Muḥammad Sarwar, Lahore, 1948

Beck, Theodore, "The Congress and the Muhammadans," *M.A.O. College Magazine*, March 1897, pp. 124-33

Ḥālī, Alṭāf Ḥusayn, *Maqālāt-i Ḥālī*, Vol. II, Delhi, 1943

Ḥasan, M. Mahdī, *Ifādāt-i Mahdī*, Ed. Mahdī Begam, Lahore, 1949

Ibn Farīd, Ed., *Adīb*, "Shiblī Nambar," Agra, 1960

Ikrām, Shaykh Muḥammad, *Shiblī Nāmah*, Lucknow, n.d.

Khān, Khān 'Ubayd Allāh, Ed. *Maqālāt-i Yawm-i Shiblī*, Lahore, 1961

Khān, Sayyid Aḥmad, *Ākhirī Maḍāmīn*, Lahore, 1898

——, *Maqālāt-i Sar Sayyid*, Vol. V, Lahore, 1962

——, *Mukammal Majmū'ah-i Laykcharz-o Ispīchiz, 1863-1898*, Ed. In'ām al-Dīn Gujrātī, Lahore, 1900

——, *Al-Taḥrīr fī Uṣūl al-Tafsīr*, Agra, 1892

Mahdī, Muḥammad, *Tadhkirah Shams al-'Ulamā' Mawlānā Shiblī Marḥūm*, Bombay, 1925

Manglorī, Ṭufayl Aḥmad, *Musalmānon kā Roshan Mustaqbil*, Delhi

Muḥammad, Mi'rāj, "Shāh Walī Allāh's Attempt to Reconcile the Schools of Fiqh," Unpublished M.A. Thesis, McGill University, Montreal, 1968

Nadwī, Sayyid Sulaymān, *Ḥayāt-i Shiblī*, Azamgarh, 1943

Rahman, Fazlur, *Islam*, London, 1966

Rahman, Fazlur, "Revival and Reform in Islam," *The Cambridge History of Islam*, Vol. II, Ed. P.M. Holt, *et al.*, Cambridge, 1970, pp. 632-56

Rizvi, S.A.A., "The Breakdown of Traditional Society," *The Cambridge History of Islam*, Vol. II, Ed. P.M. Holt, *et al.*, Cambridge, 1970, pp. 97-119

Safran, Nadav, *Egypt in Search of Political Community*, Cambridge, Massachusetts, 1961

Shiblī Nu'mānī, *Bāqīyāt-i Shiblī*, Lahore, 1965

——, *Al-Ghazālī*, Lahore, 1952

——, *'Ilm al-Kalām*, Agra, n.d.

——, *Al-Kalām*, Cawnpore, 1313 H.

——, *Khuṭūṭ-i Shiblī*, Ed. Muḥammad Amīn Zubayrī, Agra, n.d.

——, *Kullīyāt-i Shiblī* (Urdu), Azamgarh, 1954

——, *Makātīb*, 2 vols., Ed. Sayyid Sulaymān Nadwī, Azamgarh, 1927-28

——, *Maqālāt-i Shiblī*, Vol. I (Religious), Azamgarh, 1954

——, *Maqālāt-i Shiblī*, Vol. IV (Critical), Azamgarh, 1934

——, *Maqālāt-i Shiblī*, Vol. V, Part I (Historical), Azamgarh, 1936

——, *Maqālāt-i Shiblī*, Vol. VII (Philosophical), Azamgarh, 1938

——, *Maqālāt-i Shiblī*, Vol. VIII (Miscellaneous), Azamgarh, 1938

——, *Safarnāmah-i Rūm-o Miṣr-o Shām*, Azamgarh, 1940

——, *Sawāniḥ Mawlawī Rūm*, Lahore, 1909

Smith, Wilfred Cantwell, "Islam Confronted by Western Secularism: Revolutionary Reaction," *Islam in the Modern World*, Ed. Dorothea Seelye Franck, Washington, D.C., 1951, pp. 19-30

Smith, Wilfred Cantwell, *Islam in Modern History*, Princeton, 1957

——, *Modern Islam in India*, Lahore, 1969

Zubayrī, Muḥammad Amīn, *Dhikr-i Shiblī*, Lahore, 1953

Index

Index

Index